Narrative Art

Art News Annual XXXVI

Narrative Art

Edited by Thomas B. Hess and John Ashbery

The Macmillan Company,
New York

Like so much narrative art, the untitled
drawing at left by Saul Steinberg (see article
on page 52) is obviously telling a story,
but what is it? The special pleasures and
problems of story-telling art, from Egyptian
underground murals to today's underground comics,
are discussed in this volume of Art News Annual.
The cover is a montage of drawings, about 8 feet
high by Steinberg (photo, Eric Pollitzer).

Art News Annual XXXVI

Managing Editor	Elizabeth C. Baker
Executive Editor	Harris Rosenstein
Senior Editor	Henry A. La Farge
Associate Editor	Dolores Fenn
Editorial Associate	Joyce Clarke
Design Director	Bradbury Thompson
Production Manager	Angelo Cutro
Production Assistant	Robert Preato
Publisher	Alvin Garfin
Advertising Sales	Sephine B. Melrod, Marian Conner
Advertising Assistant	Sarah K. Brigham
Circulation	Harriet Albert

Art News Annual (incorporating Portfolio)
is published each October by Newsweek, Inc.
444 Madison Avenue, New York, N.Y. 10022

Art News Annual is distributed for
Newsweek, Inc. by The Macmillan Company,
866 Third Avenue, New York, N.Y. 10022

Narrative Art

Contents

Pieter Brueghel the Elder: *The Painter and the Connoisseur,* ca. 1565,
pen and brown ink, 9 3/4 inches high. Albertina, Vienna. The drawing
immediately attracted attention, as four contemporary copies of it are known.

By Lawrence Gowing

Brueghel's World

**The ultimate fable behind this sixteenth-century master's
catalogues of games and tortures, beggars and kings,
is nothing less than a natural history of modern humanity**

There is a special mood for looking at the great artists who
have faced the worst or glorified the best. You set out for
Colmar or Rome and prepare for them to take dramatic pos-
session of you, at least until the holiday is over. At home it
is all quite different; one is out of reach of dramatizations.
But suppose that after breakfast, when the bathroom is occupied by children and one is carrying a paperback that has on
its cover Michelangelo's mask of deceitful dream from *Night,*
one makes for a lavatory outside which is inconveniently
small. So small that finding hung over the paper because
there is nowhere else—there is never an alternative to the way
things are—a child's toilet-seat like the peaked hat of a hunting saint complete with chinstrap, it may just occur to one,
while still keeping track of Michelangelo's remark that every
human habit, dress, dwelling and persona is a kind of painting, that the place to rest the thing for a moment is on one's
head. That is how the awareness dawns, while children take
turns with a hobby-horse wheel and stamp about outside.
Only Brueghel has known how it is in actual life.

Others imagined the grandeur and terror, but he knew the
grotesque normality. We owe to him the capacity of art to
deal with incongruity and indignity and to see a little of the
sense and nonsense of man's situation in the real world.
Brueghel offers a vision of man at the mercy of his fantasy
and folly, inextricably involved with his fellows and an inseparable part of the material world, dwarfed by the earth. He
saw these circumstances all together and spelt them out
quite plainly in the great paintings that everyone knows.

Yet the familiarity and the legibility are deceptive. You can
never be sure that you have finally construed one of these
crowded scenes. They have sometimes the character of

Author: Lawrence Gowing, painter, head of the art department at
England's progressive University of Leeds, has written books on
Vermeer, Turner, Matisse; he contributes frequently to *Art News.*

crowds, perhaps in preference to the conventional character
of art. Brueghel surely knew the description of an ancient
Greek painter that Ortelius, the Humanist geographer who
was Brueghel's friend, quoted in his obituary: "When asked
which of his predecessors he followed he pointed to a crowd
of people and said it was nature herself whom one ought to
imitate, not an artist." Brueghel may well have recognized
himself; he would have liked the identification of a crowd
as nature.

The various and eccentric shape of man, the social confusion, the fantasy and vice—all these were included in his
view. Idealization, reasoning and measure on the other hand
were conspicuously absent. There was no sign of the heroic
formula for the human body that other painters brought back
from Italy, no ornament, no added charm to spoil the likeness. "Of such blemishes," Ortelius wrote, "our friend Brueghel was perfectly free."

Instead Brueghel brought back from Italy a stored-up
vision of the landscape that he had passed through on the
way. His contemporaries said that he swallowed the mountains whole and vomited them up again into his pictures;
there is indeed an impression in the great drawings, which
hardly anyone knows but specialists, of something indigest-
ible embodied entire. It is something larger, reflecting back
less of human preoccupation, something more foreign to man
than even Leonardo or Dürer had conceived before. Not that
it is always grand or intimidating. After the great rocks, in
the next sheet a nondescript Italian hill lies vaporous and fra-
grant in the sun. Often the scene follows a pattern from Venice or Antwerp. The sense which Brueghel brought back was
a sense of naturalness, the sense in every form and mood of
nature of a generative force quite separate and distinct from
man.

When Brueghel settled down to draw for the engravers in
Antwerp, he characterized mankind with equal force. It was
not the individual that he drew but the species and its com-

mon consistency, the diversity and the uniformity of the crowd. It is another kind of naturalness; Brueghel's starting point was the separate definition of man and nature, an antithesis as absolute as good and evil. To summarize in the briefest way the area of his subsequent achievement, one could say that he proceeded to show nature *in* man, and then thirdly (and almost finally) the place of man in nature. Yet the words tell nothing. Applied to Brueghel they are oddly tautologous; perhaps it is because the common way we visualize this huge terminology—*nature, man*—is to a significant degree due to Brueghel himself and to the pervasive influence that is with us still.

Ortelius' view of his friend was much like ours. He used to speak of Brueghel's pictures as he tells us (I quote Fritz Grossmann's translation of the document from Wolfgang Stechow's anthology) "as hardly works of art but as works of Nature. Nor should I call him the best of painters but rather the very nature of painters."

Developing conceptions of nature echo continually through Brueghel's imagery. The nature in man made itself visible from the start in the variety of behavior and the rank abundance of fantasy. Both were grotesque, and both could be scanned for symbolic signs of the significance of life. Contemporaries who knew Brueghel by his prints regarded him as a follower of Bosch; very likely he regarded himself as such. The vein of fantasy that he pursued dated from two generations earlier; Bosch had died some 10 years before Brueghel was born. The *Painter and Patron* in Brueghel's famous drawing were figures from the past and the theme is the timeless difference between the integrity and the fortitude of the man who produces art and the myopic worldliness of the one whose only function is to dip into his purse and pay for it.

The fantastic imagery of the early sixteenth century opened to visual awareness a range of connotations that were otherwise unconfessed (a range that, despite the art of this century, has now in some respects contracted) and Brueghel took full advantage of it. Nevertheless, there is a gulf between him and Bosch. In the encounters with the supernatural that Bosch painted mankind was the fragile and vulnerable victim. Brueghel's demons have whimsically suicidal eccentricities but the real power for evil rests with man. In the climate of thought inspired by Erasmus, follies of the mind no longer belong to the Devil. On the contrary, the fantasies that exemplify Brueghel's *Mortal Sins* have a fertility that is positively delightful. The sardonic inversion is complete when, a year or two later, Brueghel illustrates the *Virtues* and finds them one and all to be imposed by theology, deformed by society or traduced by the conditions of human life. Prudence is cowardice, Justice is torture, Faith is observance while Charity is simply misplaced and Temperance is ignorant incompetence in the liberal arts.

In the engravings Brueghel was certainly catering to more than one level of sophistication, and a sadistic taste is a common feature of the popular appetite for moralizing prints. But the irony is unquestionable. If Brueghel's later meaning is problematic it is because of the difficulty that we find in relating this sardonic complexity, which we must often suspect below the surface, with a significance that is beyond a doubt directly visual, true and undivided. When we have a problem with an artist it is usually in essence his own problem. The conventions that Brueghel confronted had in truth

The Large Rhine Landscape, ca. 1553-54, pen and ink, 13 5/8 inches high. The Pierpont Morgan Library, New York.

The Return of the Herd (November?), 1556, 46 inches high (below and detail right), one of Brueghel's Series of the Months, commissioned for a scheme of decoration in a palatial house in Antwerp. Kunsthistorisches Museum, Vienna.

Pride, from the series of engravings after Brueghel on the Mortal Sins; it illustrates
the proverb "Where pride and luxury lead the way, shame and poverty bring up the rear."

a frightful power. The issues round which the ambiguous allegories revolve are those that divided the Netherlands and the Christian world. The best of Brueghel's engravers was within 20 years to die horribly at the hands of Spanish soldiers.

It would be pleasant to agree with Auden:

> About suffering they were never wrong
> The Old Masters: how well they understood
> Its human position; how it takes place
> While somebody is eating or opening a window or just
>   walking dully along...

But actually the view of suffering that the Mannerist and Baroque masters in general shared with their society seems to mix complacency with equivocation. Brueghel's eventual awareness of suffering is revealed precisely in the degree that it receives undivided attention. The customary interpretation of *Icarus* is anachronistic:

> In Brueghel's *Icarus*, for instance: how everything
>   turns away
> Quite leisurely from the disaster; the ploughman may
> Have heard the splash, the forsaken cry,
> But for him it was not an important failure...

It is in fact hard to be sure that Icarus was much more important to Brueghel than to the plowman. On the surface the

similar details that he inserted in designs for prints merely gave subjects of low rank an attractive mythological trimming. To gather the full meaning we have to recognize that Brueghel's descriptions of human action on land and sea have always an admonitory accompaniment, symbolic at first, but more and more explicit, to remind us of the limitations of man's power. Auden was in no mood to recognize it when reportage was regarded as the basic virtue of art and his later title for the poem, *Musée des Beaux Arts,* confesses that its subject was a line of talk in a picture gallery rather than artistic truth. Icarus and Phaëthon may mean pride, impiety and disobedience but hardly suffering. When the reality of suffering appears in Brueghel's world his reaction is far less philosophical and more moral.

A certain sardonic independence was, to judge by the allegories, the only recourse in the crisis of values, the alternative to violence and despair. That was the foundation he built on, joining simple form and color together to gather an elementary assurance of unity. Surveying the ways of man on land and sea, he found a common shape, the bellying and returning line that is common to the furrow and the sail. The unobtrusiveness of the incident of Icarus was entirely traditional. It was the normal way of peopling a landscape among the followers of Patinir (the other source of Brueghel's picture-type, who was also dead before he was born). The imaginative scope was there already, the prospect over land and water through turquoise air and the rocks like a virtuoso cadenza punctuating the melodious continuum of space. A parable, a miracle or a group listening to the Baptist—all but the regulation worldly man, who reappears in Brueghel—all these are in themselves incidental, sometimes hardly noticeable until you search, and then you are as likely to find an owl. But not superfluous; they complete the compendium of the world's contents, maybe supplying a spark of fire to join the elements of earth, water and air, in any case an integral part of the world-picture conveying a spiritual dimension.

The position that Brueghel's later pictures accorded to landscape in its own right was no more predominant than it had become in the panels of Patinir's supposed nephew Herri, the owl specialist, whose half-naïve *pointillé* touch with foliage already gave an atmospheric vibration to the scene. The tradition of compendious, undifferentiated presentation was reflected equally in the Northern illustrative method. Brueghel's Christ carrying the Cross was no more lost in the unfeeling crowd than in the versions by Herri long before. Finally, to complete the list of ingredients that are usually credited to Brueghel, the mid-sixteenth century saw an efflorescence of large-scale genre painting by artists like Pieter Aertsen, with peasant feasts, dancing to the bagpipes, pride, gluttony and lust. It is quite like Brueghel, from the emblematic feathers in the hat to the bulging codpieces, and also, when one encounters Aertsen's personification of morality, looking out at the audience with comic chagrin, quite unlike him in all significant respects.

The way that Brueghel embodied all this material in something that transcends the terms of art is one of the wonders of the European achievement. Ortelius' impression of it as a work of nature was not altogether fanciful. In Brueghel's three seminal masterpieces, *Proverbs, The Battle of Carnival and Lent* and *Children's Games,* the all-over scattering of figures dispersed like flotsam shows less apparent design than anything else in art. For a good reason: instead of design Brueghel equipped himself with a method. Each picture is an exhaustive collection of all the miscellaneous behavior observable in a specific connection. The sections of life have one thing in common; they are those in which people behave in formalized, habitual ways, ways that can be labeled, listed and reconstructed. One picture takes the cross-section on a specific day, Ash Wednesday. The forms of behavior recorded are festive customs and habitual reactions to them. Another takes the section at a certain age, childhood, and catalogues the 85 varieties of play. A third picture selects a particular aspect, verbal behavior, the kind of behavior that labels itself; it reconstructs the content of clichés and saws reflecting universal attitudes and fantasies no painter could invent.

Brueghel's way was characteristic of a time when the varieties of behavior, verbiage and play were seen as prodigious in themselves. But so far from cherishing what was fabulous in life, in the manner of Rabelais with his list of the infant Gargantua's games, Brueghel saw nothing very splendid in the facts; even dealing with fantasy the value of his account is its sober truth. There were one or two precedents of an elementary kind for the *Proverbs,* and *Carnival and Lent* had been painted, no doubt quite differently, by Bosch. The intellectual climate of Antwerp favored the encyclopedic comprehensiveness of Brueghel's method; Ortelius had begun to compile the maps that were eventually collected in the first atlas of the world and Plantin was to produce the Polyglot Bible in the same years. Brueghel's series represents none the less a marvelous stroke of methodology, such

Children's Games, 1560, 46½ inches high.
Kunsthistorisches Museum, Vienna.

Landscape with the Fall of Icarus, ca. 1555,
Musées Royaux des Beaux-Arts, Brussels.

The Tower of Babel, 1563, 44 7/8 inches high (Kunsthistorisches Museum, Vienna) was evidently inspired by the Colosseum. This seems confirmed by a very small early version on ivory, now lost, painted by Brueghel during his stay in Rome around 1554, as recorded in the inventory of the Roman miniaturist Giulio Clovio.

as originality at large perhaps depends on. Not merely in art; these pictures, which invented an order of image and opened a whole visual territory to painting, devising quite incidentally the method of social anthropology as well, have a larger importance in the life of man.

Brueghel's breakthrough was possibly a realization that the matter of fantasy has an actual existence in the light of day. Awareness of the comic incongruity of figures of speech again is not uncommon in the sixteenth century. It is Brueghel's understanding that the comedy reflects real predicaments that is exceptional. One can start on the proverbs anywhere; on the left the eye is caught by the white shirt of the man who runs his *head against the wall.* The literalness of the visual translation makes suicidal obstinacy real. The man will *die in harness* and he is accordingly buckled into armor. The associations gather momentum; his head in its stone-colored cap is halfway to wall-color and following the impetus we come to the personification of futile bellicosity *armed to the teeth.* Quite literally, for he bites on iron, *on a bullet* as we say (not many of the proverbs need much translating). He is a parody of courage; he is *belling the cat,* fumbling with a bell that is

incongruously large. It is almost the only point at which Brueghel distorts the literal reconstruction, just as Magritte might distort it and in the same interest, the dream-like potential of the same kind of bell. They belong to the same culture and nothing dies in art.

As the associations proliferate the wall becomes one side of a stone-colored dwelling for a whole vocabulary of follies. The pugnacious cocks on the next ledge are eluding a miserable visionary who *counts his chickens before they are hatched.* Further on there is a cell for the duplicity that *speaks with two mouths;* the face is hideously cleft. Then the fantasy breaks loose into a fatuous dream. The inside of the house becomes bright and out staggers an idiot with his burden, steaming like soup; he is bringing *basketfuls of light into day,* like coals to Newcastle. The shining doorway is magical, like Magritte's reversals of day and night, and an Italianate tabernacle is built on to the house to shelter the perverse associations. Under the pink canopy one man *lights candles to the devil;* another *has the devil for a confessor,* and so on. As one follows the train of thought one realizes what is being represented so graphically. Men are saddled with these formula-

The Triumph of Death, ca. 1562, 46 inches high (Prado, Madrid) was described by Brueghel's biographer, the contemporary Flemish humanist Karel van Mander, as a painting "in which expedients of every kind are tried out against death."

The Netherlandish Proverbs, 1559, 46 inches high (below and details right), State Museums, Berlin, in which about 100 proverbs have been identified.

The Proverb of the Bird's Nest, 1568, 23¼ inches high. Kunsthistorisches Museum, Vienna.

tions precisely because they are the captives of propensities too vicious, mad or boring to be spelt out *en clair*. When we meet the peasant in the white shirt again on the right of the picture we discover the practical consequence. *He cannot reach from one loaf to another*—he does not know where his next meal is coming from. He falls forward across the table, crucified by hunger.

The method leads Brueghel to look directly, among the proverbial follies and vices, at a commonplace fact of the human condition. The survey is quite neutral, as if statistical; as one might say, 3.2 per cent of clichés assume the existence of starvation and (right in the middle) the hopeless futility of labor. Only the conjunction of misery with silliness and sin points a kind of conclusion: the 125 clichés are so many ways in which men are the victims of their own frame of mind.

The other picture that Brueghel painted in the same year, *Carnival and Lent,* took a sample from a specific time and place. However scrupulous one is to look at it without hindsight and with no more sentiment than Brueghel himself, one can hardly doubt the signs that he was directly concerned, as painting had never been before, with the material and moral conditions of actual life.

The time is Ash Wednesday and the place a market square. Carnival, played by a butcher pushed on his sledge by a pot-man, jousts with the emaciated simpleton playing Lent (the very model for a Mannerist saint), who is pulled by a monk and a nun. Behind them the opposing forces of urban life divide. Siding with Carnival on the left there is debauchery and general tomfoolery, play-acting and fornication, with idiocy, callousness and a certain amount of enjoyment mingled together. On the opposite side, by the church, there is observance, piety, the religious life and the sober laity, with charity and mercy and some vain repetition and hypocrisy as well. One can read back and forth across the picture or up

and down for as long as one can bear the most appalling images of poverty, mutilation and despair that exist in art. In fact Brueghel has spared us a little; he painted over a naked body, dead from starvation in front of the pious procession, with a cloth.

This is the truest painting of poverty because it is informed with its ironies—the insignificance of charity, the impossibility of weighing need. Who is the pregnant woman to deprive? What can the solicitous burgher do in the face of infinite agony when the beggars who press forward are the frauds? And so on; there is no verdict. On the whole the maimed and stricken are worse neglected under the aegis of Carnival. The religious, when all is said and done, are not entirely wrapped up in themselves. Yet Brueghel is dealing here, and in some sense in almost every picture after, with wider issues. Reading across from side to side the question is: what is so Christian about a Christian society? Or reading up and down from the establishments to the havoc in their shadow: in this vale of tears isn't any social order a contradiction in terms? There is no sign that either question has lost its urgency nor that any consideration has a better chance of engaging attention than Brueghel's.

The baffling behavior of men requires complex interpretation; children act out the patterns of life for themselves. Brueghel shows them self-absorbed in trance-like realization of companionship and competition, solidarity in common dreams, mimic cruelty, automatic joy. They rehearse the business of life together; separately they explore qualities of person and thing. Even those who are occupied on their own, like the gymnasts in their paddock and the turd-stirrer in the middle, are linked invisibly to the rest. The picture is a portrayal of social cohesion, with its radial tensions and circular organization. It shows the congregation of individuals into groups which then gravitate together—yet not quite together,

The Hunters in the Snow (below and detail left), 1565, 46 inches high, January in Brueghel's Series of the Months. Kunsthistorisches Museum, Vienna.

The Massacre of the Innocents, ca. 1565-67, 45 5/8 inches high. Kunsthistorisches Museum, Vienna.

for Brueghel has an exact sense of the elbowroom that human beings allow one another—into the aggregate that makes a society. The momentum that holds each child as if in orbit is the quality of life in a culture that was already immensely ancient and it is altered only superficially today.

The view of childhood is the only part of Brueghel's survey that discovers any kind of comfort. The mimic flagellation of a top against a pillar is the barest reference; playing at churches is relegated to a corner and we need not believe that the children around the distant bonfire, the last game that we discover and the most ominous, think of it as a burning at the stake. But we know for sure how happy the agreements of children are; the pair of red skirts whose wearers play at "milling about" fairly spin together against the turquoise grass. The relief at turning away from the adult world is perceptible and Brueghel chose a style to suit. Or rather, he chose a kind of abstinence from style. In place of oil paint he used tempera, the medium of medieval tradition; it retains all its clarity today. By contrast with the sophisticated stylistic weaponry of convention, his procedure was increasingly guileless and childlike. The concision and directness of the manner that he evolved in *Children's Games* remained in all his later work.

Each part has its decided, simple shape, which realizes the form with a minimum of modeling, and its specific hue established with the least amount of paint from a limited range of clear colors that are always distinct. A greenish-blue for garments and the sky also makes the bluish-green of vegetation. A pale, flat cinnabar red, which occasionally produces a neutral pink for a loose cloak or a flapping flag in later pictures, is darkened only a little to make brick. The buff ocher that is the ground of everything is sometimes sharpened into yellow. Later it shades into brown for sodden earth and cows. There is grey, black and white. That is all. No color predominates; their intensity is about equal and there is an equality in their pictorial status. Each is present or latent everywhere, to crop up at any moment and add another shape to its alliance. None of them is missing for long.

A picture by Brueghel is mapped out in widespread federations of color, distributed with an elementary and perfect grace. Looking into the scene we find that it embraces incidents and figures that are graceless and a state of life that is disgraceful. The extremes of folly and vice are included, with whatever misery is visited on them, yet the ultimate impression is not dark. The customs, games and proverbs, all the institutions of popular life, are forms of a common creativeness. We become aware of the imaginative resourcefulness of human adjustments. The wryness and the fatalism, linked to the perfect counterpoint of the visual scheme, are forms of reconciliation to fate and nature—even to the unnatural nature of man. Naïve delight and viciousness alike, the wealth of fantasy and actual destitution, are all incorporated side by side.

The comprehensive image gives an assurance of a basic unity which is at first sight inexplicable, if not inappropriate. Perhaps at root it is this that visitors to the Vienna museum enjoy. The comic and the fearful are combined in a characteristic form with which we are at ease. Coming on Brueghel people smile; they always did. Within a year or two commentators were remarking on the fact. To judge by recent interpreters the indictment should have made them weep. In the years following *Children's Games* Brueghel extended his view to folklore, with the harridan who defies the world and hell as well, and to a survey of every variety of mortality and cruelty in a *Triumph of Death* on the medieval model. It was like a presentiment of what was in store a few years later. Yet even the vast panorama of doom is contained in a scheme that is in essence gentle (it is the Italianate inferno of Floris that is sadistic).

The detachment and reserve of Brueghel's standpoint and the abrupt tenderness that goes with it are often at odds with his apparent theme. However we construe the emblematic meaning of his monkeys, whether we read more of greed or spiritual blindness or despair, it is clear enough that their captivity in the monkey condition is likened to the imprisonment of man in the human condition. Yet the picture is not satirical. Alone in monkey imagery these animals are vehicles of sympathy. Without abating the diagnosis of human failings in the least, their melancholy beauty encourages us to feel pity and love for living things and men amongst them.

The Proverb of the Bird's Nest illustrates a typically cynical rustic saw: "He who knows where the nest is has the knowledge; he who robs it has the nest." Brueghel reverses it. The wise fool who fails to act in self-interest, so far from despicable, is beautiful. He is the noblest figure painted by Brueghel and the most sympathetic; some think he has a look of Michelangelo's *Risen Christ*. It is the dynamic hero of the proverb who is despised; it is not even certain that he is good enough at climbing to get the nest. But that is not the end; just as we are ready to conclude that Brueghel is an enemy of selfishness and protector of birds, we realize that at the bottom of the picture the meaning is reversed again. The new hero, full of his wisdom, is about to step into the ditch. So he is the fool after all, or perhaps they both are. It is all set in so natural a landscape and one that so naturally accommodates man—a meadow bordered by little oaks with a farm where poultry feed and birds hang in the air above them waiting while the horses go to the stable and a woman carries the milk home— that the enigmatic outcome is oddly harmonious. Whether or not one code of conduct is more profitable or attractive than another, they exist for ever side by side like parts of an ecological pattern, integral parts of the countryside.

One cannot doubt that Brueghel's purpose is moral, yet the morality has a continual and curious tendency to cancel out. Certainly suffering is abhorrent; it is the ultimate, infinite evil. Yet the red horsemen who massacre the Innocents and conduct Christ to Golgotha are as human as anyone else. Brueghel's position on the religious issue is notoriously difficult to discern. The Catholic Church is shown dispensing charity and the picture of the Baptist preaching in the open air dates from the Calvinist resurgence, but there is no sign of commitment to either. The figures whose role in the action

Brueghel's largest painting, *The Procession of Christ to Golgotha*, 1564, 48 3/4 inches high, is mentioned among the 16 works by the artist owned by his rich patron in Antwerp, Niclaes Jonghelinck, in 1566. Kunsthistoriches Museum, Vienna.

The Storm at Sea, 27 5/8 inches high, in which the ship is saved by the frivolity of the whale. Kunsthistorisches Museum, Vienna.

is meanest are more than once shown to wear a crucifix and among the Baptist's hearers it is noticeable that the anxious, alienated face of the gentleman who is having his fortune told by a satanic gipsy (against Calvin's instructions) is at least as sympathetic as the simple piety around him.

We should have little use for Brueghel if his detachment were found to diminish his concern. The impression is just the reverse. The company on the way to Golgotha is climbing a muddy slope up out of the town; where the roads part there is a rock with a windmill. The chance that brings the heterogeneous crowd and the prisoners together on the path to the local execution place, while others hurry darkly away down the other road, seems as unaccountable as the winds that blow. Whichever way they blow the mill will grind; destiny will be fulfilled. There is much more interest in the current human drama—in the thieves, white with fear, and the hopeless endeavors of an optimistic Franciscan and a Dominican to confess them in a cart which is stuck in the swamp. Still more in Simon of Cyrene, and his wife who with beads and crucifix struggles to prevent him being taken to help with the Cross. Yet she is no more the enemy than are the redcoats; Brueghel's concern is with the totality, the whole condition of life as it is lived.

Very likely Brueghel took the same view of the fearful crisis of the time as Ortelius—quoted in Colin Clair's life of Plantin—who compared the Netherlands to a sick man in danger of collapse "from such various sicknesses as the Catholic evil, the Gueux fever of the insurgent resistance, the Huguenot dysentery and also plagued by black horsemen and soldiers." The last picture, *Storm at Sea*, seems to illustrate how it felt to live in the Netherlands, caught, as Ortelius described himself "between the tides of occupation and the storms." But the point turns out to be as ironical as ever: it is not due to any virtue in man that this ship is preserved in

the sea of troubles, but simply to the frivolity of the whale who goes after a barrel instead (as in *A Tale of a Tub*). The application of the emblem is sardonic in itself; the whale signifies the stupidity of missing the true good for the sake of futile trifles. But the whale's true good would have been the destruction of the ship, and no doubt of half the congregation from the church on the horizon. What can be truly good in this green flux, which makes the red of the barrel so deceptively exquisite?

Yet if art convinces one of anything, it is that this great painter's meaning is not sardonic at all. On the contrary it is single-minded; it is about *wholeness*. It is a straight portrayal of the unity that embraces all the contradictions of the world, even the deadly conflicts of man. One could believe such impressions were imaginary if there were not evidence of a viewpoint close to this among Brueghel's friends. The doctrines of the Family of Love, the secret sect to which Plantin and Ortelius and virtually all their friends belonged, set the divisions between men at nought. Its founder Hendrik Niclaes called all "lovers of truth of whatever Nation and religion soever they be, Christian, Jews, Mahomites or Turks and Heathen" to join in a fellowship of peace, abandoning contention over dogma. The sect had no rites or doctrines. Ceremonies had no meaning, except to the stupid. Beliefs might be useful, Plantin wrote, to the spiritually immature but they were inseparable from pretense and hostility. It was immaterial which church members belonged to; they might observe Catholic or Protestant practices, according to where they lived. Remain in the church if you will, Niclaes taught, or leave it if you will, it is all the same. One remembers the distant landscape of the *Proverbs*. Beside a laborer who is so hungry that *he sees the bears dancing*, a tonsured priest *hangs his cowl on the fence*, that is to say abandons holy orders. The man struggling in the river who finds that *it is hard to swim*

Submerged in its real-life setting is the *Adoration of the Kings*, or *Epiphany*, 1567, 13 3/4 inches high. Oskar Reinhart Collection, Winterthur.

The Holy Family, also called *Adoration of the Kings*, 1564, 43 3/4 inches high. National Gallery, London.

against the stream is a Franciscan. Behind, a boy who might come from Giorgione is deep in reverie on no graver problem than *who knows why the geese go barefoot?* It is all the same. When the heart is right, all else is.

The testimony in favor of liberty and against persecution appealed to many whose orthodoxy was undoubted. The Family of Love spanned the division that was tormenting Europe. For a time both iconoclasm and repression were seen to be equally mistaken. There was a nostalgia for the internationalism and the toleration of the declining Middle Ages, when it appeared that *to seek truth and utter what one believes to be true can never be a crime.* The dialogue (as Bernard Rekers has discovered) extended to the Escorial itself; in retrospect its boldness is astonishing. It ignored national divisions as if language had never been confounded and the people scattered abroad. Brueghel's *Tower of Babel* surely celebrates the doomed ideal of understanding among men. As usual the men concerned emerge without honor; the foreground illustrates the folly of abasing oneself before kings. The picture evokes the mood in which later Arias Montano, whom Philip II sent to supervise the Polyglot Bible —one of the *pompiers* of intellectual history who caught fire—would sit with Plantin and his colleagues after dinner discussing the origin of language.

Brueghel's designs often look like meditations on the tragedy of people scattered on the face of the earth, and it is significant that he illustrated no story more often than the Tower of Babel, the story that would in Humanist eyes reflect

little credit on the deity of the established order. The Antwerp intellectuals were well placed to see the tragedy of the modern world. In the Netherlands the people had been one; just as in Babel, nothing would have been restrained from them which they had imagined to do. Everything was better there—every kind of scholarship, art, technology and industry. It is no wonder that visitors from Spain were astonished and converted. Everything was in favor of a faith that confirmed Erasmus' common-sense; commitment in itself was far from being a virtue while any alternative however equivocal was open. The sailors in Brueghel's storm were stupid to set sail; Plantin compared himself to a mariner who "does not obstinately seek to cleave through the great waves but prudently avoids them with reefed sails." If there is a quality of archaism in Brueghel's art (which makes it unfashionable among art historians at the moment) it may be because a connoisseur of folly could see that the committed, progressive forces of the time were moving towards eighty years of Hell.

The only teaching of the Family of Love was the impossibility of human beings completely to understand the Bible. Christ was no longer to be looked on as an historical personage, but as a "condition" common to those who live in union with God. The context accounts for a quality in Brueghel's imagery that seems at once both inscrutable and appropriate. The Christian themes, Epiphany and the bearing of the Cross, have an oddly insubstantial existence among the vivid life around them. They appear pallid, almost transparent; rather than happenings, they are seen as institutions too, existing more in imagination than in the flesh, and thus existing perpetually, most of all in one's own time, affecting real behavior and suffering the actual weather. In the London picture a Holy Family so withdrawn, so veiled and inward looking that it scarcely seems to be present in the flesh, is adored by grotesquely characterized monarchs; there is the barest indication in the emblems of the elements on Jasper's cloak that it is the natural world that pays its incongruous tribute here.

The sense of inscrutable meaning in Brueghel's art is never so strong as when color of the simplest delicacy embraces the most cruelly fateful parts of his subject. The Cardinal in *The Triumph of Death,* supported by his own private Death, svelte as a whippet, who has the hat too, staggers towards his fate. He wears a cloak of the cool blue that is reserved for the most serene correspondences; it falls on him like a visible compassion. Niclaes called men of every kind and creed to be incorporated into the body of Christ; it is certain that this mystical essence of the "Joyful Message" was not painted or paintable. But the currency of such an idea of incorporation irrespective of difference might have encouraged a direction of thought that was far from mystical. The vast variety of *Children's Games,* all the opposing directions and minute collisions notwithstanding, is incorporated into a single pictorial substance. One is aware of a unity inherent in the existence of man, which embraces even the obdurate and miserable unawareness of it.

There was no real chance of conciliation. Resistance and repression intensified; heresy was hunted more fiercely than ever and Plantin only saved his press by arranging a bankruptcy. Brueghel's prospective mother-in-law insisted on his moving to Brussels, supposedly to break up a liaison in Antwerp; possibly the biographer misunderstood what he was

Three studies, on the left a cripple, on the right a soldier, after 1560, pen and brown ink over red chalk. Boymans-van Beuningen Museum, Rotterdam.

told and her real purpose was to get him away from the *Huis der Liefde,* the Family of Love. In the year in which Alba crossed the Alps with his army, Brueghel painted the *Conversion of St. Paul.* Yet there is no evident reference; the point is a general one. Human pride and aggression are dwarfed in the mountains and brought to a standstill by the unknown. The protagonists of force are found to be unimaginably remote in their fiercely epicene, high-waisted tailoring—the eternal military style. There is not a face to be seen, until we reach the sergeant, turning in an agony of incomprehension, half-gagged by his own steel chin-piece; we almost hear his strangled parade-ground shout. The men by contrast are formlessly bulky and inoffensive if not innocent. If anyone is ever to blame in Brueghel, it is not the rank and file; an army is a host of steel particles streaming out along magnetic lines of force. A soldier boy quite near the conversion and quite unaware of it, stands like a helmeted toadstool on the edge of the precipice. Something inexplicable happened in the mountains and even in the sergeant's mess they hardly knew that it had laid low the nastiness of the race.

Visual understanding and the reverse, visual estrangement, must always have preoccupied Brueghel. A few painters through the centuries illuminate the respect in which painting is normally a stage and the figures in it willing actors by making us aware of the reverse, the fact that painting and the painted are nothing of the kind, the sense in which both are outside our comprehension. For many years Brueghel drew the countrymen who came to market. He belonged himself to quite a different milieu. To see weddings and feasts in the country, we are told in the most significant of the stories about him, he had to dress up as a peasant. The market drawings are inscribed without exception *naar het leven,* from the life. Most of the figures that he noted were drawn from behind, turned away from him or looking down, busy with something and unaware of what was happening. A reserved man will find it difficult to look at and draw people as closely as he did in any other way, and Brueghel was known for his reserve. Most discover a more comfortable basis for imagery, but the special value to Brueghel of the contact with life is attested by the invariable inscription. He was in no danger of forgetting how the drawings were done; the inscriptions were like triumphant certificates. He often drew the figure again from in front, but the effect is less convincing. Usually it looks like a reconstruction done after the model moved away.

The later pictures often revolve round the issue of whether we can look into faces and know them. Often the faces are shut off, turned away or hidden under some hat or basket that may seem virtually to become the head, so that we get basket-headed bee-keepers, cherry-headed farm women, a pot-headed drinker, a hat-headed drunk. Brueghel did not paint from his drawings; only the reverse of a single sheet (and I have doubts about that) is directly related to a picture. The life-drawings, like the landscape drawings, were ends in themselves: they were independent enactments of naturalness, a quality quite apart from comprehension, as likely to reside in separation and the otherness of which Adrian Stokes wrote 30 years ago in some of the best pages on Brueghel that exist. With these veiled and averted heads we have a symbolic intimacy that we cannot gain, for example, from the fully visible yet strangely wilful and obdurate trio of hay-making girls in the picture of *July*. The girls are comprehensible enough; the hay to which they have chosen to devote themselves is transitory vanity, and turning their backs on the cherry harvest they have abandoned the sweetness of Paradise: their path leads towards the sharpened scythe. But this is perhaps exactly the kind of conventional moralizing that the Antwerp followers of Niclaes would have despised as only fit for fools. Looking again one sees that the cherry carriers, becoming more and more basket-headed as they recede into the distance, are at least equally diminished by their role, and also, one might imagine, by their dependence on the hutch-like image of the Virgin on a post beside them. There is no more true piety in it than in the windmill; it will be torn down soon enough when the winds of iconoclasm next blow this way. It may be that the picture has no moral except that conventional piety and obtuse worldliness are both equally facts of life. They exist side by side as naturally as a season brings both hay and cherries. Both are insignificant in themselves, except as parts of the continuum of nature. There is no alternative to the way things are.

The herdsmen in the *Return of the Herd* are embedded in nature as if inlaid: they are flat patches in the natural pattern, differing types of the identical autumnal stuff. It is their humanity, their lumpish capacity for sensation and purpose that makes them bury themselves in the picture. The only eye that meets ours is the wide innocent eye of the cow. Whatever their record on violence the Old Masters were never wrong about animals. A cow or two in the returning herd clamber frantically up slippery banks beside the path and then slither miserably down again and make off with a hobbling skip of resentment and relief. The *Hunters* are followed by a motley assemblage of dogs. Peering among them against the glare of the snow we recognize one or two that are faithful enough to hunt with; the rest are out for themselves. A single complex arabesque of pattern links them to the men, who are also out for themselves. They are all creatures of the same kind, shambling along among the upright trees. Yet not of quite the same kind; only a man is silly enough to light a bonfire where it will blow straight in the door and burn his animals' straw.

The Old Masters were right because observing animals they saw a touchstone of man's awareness of the community of living things. Brueghel made it visible; a sense of life that man did not possess before and will not entirely lose again develops from picture to picture. The birds supply their own distinct commentary. Nothing is more indicative than the human attitude to them. The childish birdtrap beside the skaters is a reminder that ice still represents as it did in Brueghel's earliest print, the perilous slipperiness of human life; if fortune is treacherous it is because children grow up to be greedy and cruel. The accord of land and sky and the orange light of coming snow embrace the scene calmly; the birds flutter and perch about and always will. Beyond the returning herd there is a birdtrap with a direr message. It is an instrument of the same kind, drawn with the same mean spidery line as the gallows and the wheel by the river beyond.

The birds are like a chorus. Each kind had its established connotation that everyone could read. In the February darkness the greedy seagull wheels in from the estuary over the village where a family are coming home from Carnival; it marks the selfishness of the man who keeps for himself the waffles that his wife and children long for. The contrast between indulgence and frugal industry was commonplace; the

The Conversion of St. Paul, 1567, 42½ inches high, was painted the year the Duke of Alba crossed the Alps. Kunsthistorisches Museum, Vienna.

Hay-Making (July), from the Series of the Months, ca. 1565. Prince Lobkowitz Collection, Raudnitz, Czechoslovakia.

The Merry Way to the Gallows, also called the *Magpie on the Gallows,* 1568, 18 1/8 inches high. Darmstadt Museum.

The Peasant Wedding, ca. 1567, 44 7/8 inches high. Kunsthistorisches Museum, Vienna.

point of the picture is to see it as part, perhaps an inevitable one, of a natural conflict that darkens the world. Nature has no moral; it can only show each creature learning or failing to learn its separate part in the harmony of the world. Of all the birds, the magpie tells most. It is the emblem of adaptability and independence; in the hard January weather poised between the mirrored tones of ice and sky, it teaches every other living thing to *se gouverner selon le temps.* Brueghel invented weather: he made it visible for the first time. But even that is not the greatest achievement of the *Months.* To a perceptible extent our visual adjustment to the natural order is due to him—and thus perhaps an attitude that makes living in a certain latitude with certain vices less cruel, less graceless. In any case, if Brueghel's standpoint is never quite learned, he will never be forgotten when it snows.

In Brueghel's last pictures the moral references are evident. There are plenty of signs of the view that feasting is greed and envy, merry-making is lust and pride. But whose view is it? The satisfactions of the flesh, to judge by the bride at the *Peasant Wedding,* are fatuously empty, but earnest conversation, clerical or lay, appears no better. Even the neglect of a holy image nailed to a tree is not in the context of iconoclasm any great reproach, any more than the pious broadsheets pinned up in the barn reflect much credit. Brueghel's view is a world away from the naïve moral comedies of Aertsen. For Brueghel the moralizing is simply a part of the subject. It is one of the propensities of man, and it is not clear that it is much less ludicrous than the rest. On the contrary, it looks laughably insignificant beside the bulk and grossness of human bodies and their coarse vigor.

Looking across the world, as Brueghel does, we see the vigor and sinfulness of the flesh against a wider perspective of human folly and natural law. A picture that he dated in the year before he died (at probably not much more than 40)

shows a crowd of revelers in the dawn eddying out of a village up to the hill towards the place where the local gibbet is installed and also, with an irony that is already sufficient, a cross, which has survived the collapse of the chapel around it. It is sometimes called *The Merry Way to the Gallows* from a proverb, but as usual the proverbial wisdom is reversed. There is no particular likelihood that dancing will lead to hanging. According to Brueghel's own comment, though again perhaps the biographer did not get the story quite right, it was the gossips who deserved to be hung.

A dancer breaks away to defecate in the bushes; one's eye travels upward to look through the cool air across a sweep of country where a great river turns towards the sea. The village dance is dwarfed by the gallows, which dwindle in their turn by contrast with the natural prospect. Only the independent, adaptable magpie has the freedom of it all. The bird's presence is possibly the sign of the only moral there is—the vice of whatever attachment leads men to kill and die. Beside the living force of nature, the death-wish that stalked across the later sixteenth century was comprehensible only as a hideous folly. Brueghel was not alone in feeling this; the mood of his revelers would have been near to the song in the Christ Church manuscript.

Hey, nonny no!
Men are fools that wish to die!
Is't not fine to dance and sing
When the bells of death do ring?
Is't not fine to swim in wine
And turn up the toe,
and sing Hey, nonny no!
When the winds blow, and the seas flow?
Hey, nonny no!

Brueghel's own view was larger and more subtle. *The Blind Leading the Blind* fall into the ditch but not through any detectable error. There is no sign that their theology is at fault (as some critics think); from their beads and crucifixes one would guess that their orthodoxy is impeccable and their observance unfailing. They are on the side of the church, which will nevertheless survive them; no doubt the village, the actual village of Pède Sainte-Anne near Brussels, is in entire agreement with them. It is the agreement that is horrible. They move as one, thay are committed and we see it to be a hideous spiritual destitution. Yet it is not merely hideous; it is also pitiful. Even though we know what was done in the name of orthodoxy, we cannot withhold compassion. And not only compassion; the counterpoint of positive hues is replaced by a rippling iridescence which assimilates the figures to the continuum of nature. Ultimately they are beautiful. The close harmony of colors calls to mind, and was perhaps intended to, the proverb that was a favorite with Erasmus: *To the blind all colors agree.*

Our capacity to follow Brueghel's comprehensive charity may be as limited as the capacity of his own time, and for the same reason. In our present struggles, a committed intolerance is as much *de rigueur* on both sides as it was then. The ideal of spiritual liberty was the creation of the sixteenth-century sects, and it will stand for ever. As the great movement developed it drew some of its imaginative dress and dwelling and its visual persona from Brueghel.

No man has contributed more to the imagery and the self-image of a society. To Room X in the Vienna museum the creatures of this same culture come from a dozen countries hour by hour to point their sharp fingers at these pictures, and trace the patterns of behavior, count them up and marvel, then point again more sharply than ever. With Brueghel painting becomes involved in the almost hopeless attempt of men to live together in their world.

The Blind Leading the Blind, 1568, 33 7/8 inches high, illustrates a parable from the Gospel of St. Matthew. National Museum, Naples.

The Peasant Dance (below and detail right), ca. 1566, 44 7/8 inches high, illustrates the climax of a village *kermess,* but with moral references to lust, anger and pride. Kunsthistorisches Museum, Vienna.

Detail of Millais' *Mariana*
(colorplate p. 30).

By George MacBeth

Subliminal Dreams

**In a period when even piano legs were disguised in
frilly knickers, artists of Victorian England introduced covert
narratives of sex and violence into their Romantic images**

In advertising, which provides so many analogues for the depth impact of narrative art, there is an available but I believe generally eschewed technique involving the insertion of extraneous frames in film sequences directly urging the purchase, or consumption, of brand goods. As the images move through the projector at the normal speed of 24 frames per second, the thinking eye fails to pick out the one frame in 24 which furtively profers the advertiser's advice, perhaps to feel thirsty for a soft drink, or hungry for a particular make of hot sausage. No doubt rightly, our liberal consciences revolt against this blow below the belt of rational approval. However, there is wisdom in reflecting how far a similar deceit, or sleight of hand, has traditionally intensified, or even first quickened, our sensuous response to some Victorian painting. Pictures in galleries remain static, as films do not, but there is a real sense in which an equivalent for this kind of "subliminal" imagery can be detected, as it were swimming, or flickering, below the apparent surface of many nineteenth-century figurative works. In much Victorian narrative painting, the story which the picture tells on the surface is a good deal less coaxingly sexy, or ambivalently violent, than the one it dwells on, and sells us, in its depths. The two stories may even be quite at variance with one another, creating a sort of tension between charm and *Angst,* as in Egg's *The Traveling Companions,* or between humor and lickerishness, as in Tissot's *Boarding The Yacht.*

In many Surrealist paintings, such as Dali's *The Persistence of Memory* or Tanguy's *The Furniture of Time,* we often seem to confront an inversion of this device. The picture can begin by seeming to mystify and titillate, as a dream does, but with the passage of time it can sometimes happen that the dream

Author: Poet George MacBeth works for the B.B.C.,
contributes to such journals as the *New Statesman*
and agitates for a revival of Augustus Egg, R.A.

may emerge as too coldly academic in its resonance, evidently aiming to illustrate quite directly some reference in an early analyst. One might begin to mount a fairly testing attack on a painter such as Delvaux along these lines. My object here, however, is rather to stress the opposing tendency of some neglected Victorian works, that seem too explicit and literary on the surface while they insidiously later reveal glimpses of a more dream-like and piercingly irrational meaning in their depths.

An excellent example of how a visual narrative can seem to be anchored in, and bounded by, a literary narrative while in fact using it only as a springboard, is offered by Millais' *Mariana,* 1851, inspired by Tennyson's poem (published in 1830). Tennyson describes a lonely, dispirited girl in the remote and barren part of the countryside he had grown up in as a child. The selection of each detail in his landscape is carefully geared to a vision of infertility as concise and terrible as Eliot's in *The Waste Land.* Tennyson's poem in no way deals with the onset, or even the aftermath, of physical love: it concerns itself entirely with its absence. It is a masterpiece, not of sexuality, but of rejection. With Millais, despite the contemporary, and I think subsequent, assumption that his work is illustrating the same theme, all this is changed. On the surface, there is a close connection between the painting and the poem. Indeed, the lines which set Millais off are said to have been the (almost effetely melancholy) refrain ones:

> *She only said, "My life is dreary,*
> *He cometh not," she said;*
> *She said, "I am aweary, aweary,*
> *I would that I were dead!"*

It could be, as my later analysis might seem to support, that Millais drew on the pun of orgasm perhaps present in the second line, but the intended flow of Tennyson's almost puritanical abstraction in the poem would hardly encourage such a reading. The visibly most fruitful phrase for Millais seems

Left: John Everett
Millais' *Mariana*,
1851, panel, 23 1/2
inches high. Collection
Lord Sherfield, London.

Right: 1968 poster,
copyright Personality
Posters, New York

clearly to have been the later and apparently more neutral "glanced athwart" in the lines:

She drew her casement-curtain by,
And glanced athwart the glooming flats.

Even a casual look will show that the central image of the picture is the sensuous twist given to Mariana's body as she drowsily inclines her head—not, however, to look out for her absent lover, but to appraise the forward young angel making the two-finger sign of sexual invitation before her very eye in the checkered glass of the Gothic window pane. The *casement-curtain* of Tennyson's moated grange is firmly drawn back, stirred up to a stiff brocade screen of beasts, birds and burgeoning fruits. The *glooming flats* of his boyhood Lincolnshire are quickened to the lush growth of a twining Oxford garden. But the girl has indeed precisely *glanced athwart* as she meets the gaze of her gilded would-be lover. The surrounding passages of the image unpack, as it were, the full implications of her muted, and yet densely mysterious, gaze. The boy in the window is, of course, the Archangel Gabriel, come to approach Mary with the news of her forthcoming sacred impregnation. The meeting of his eyes, not with those of the Virgin in the window, but with the hotter, more livingly lustful eyes of the girl in the room, pronounce the preliminary sexual arousal of a secular *Annunciation.*

In this connection one may interestingly compare Rossetti's two roughly contemporary pictures, *The Girlhood of Mary Virgin,* 1848-49, and *Ecce Ancilla Domini,* 1849-50. Both center on the elegant sinuosity of the twisted herald's

wand, watered and stroked aloft in the earlier oil by the child-like hand of the nymphet Mary, shuddered away from by her neurotic teen-age self when it is later presented in the fingers of the flame-footed messenger. The wicked lily was clearly in the Pre-Raphaelite air of the late '40s. It was certainly present in Mariana's unconscious thoughts, as the third panel of Millais' window makes us realize, offering, as it does, almost a Freudian dream of repressed feelings. Here is the tight visor of her maidenhead, perhaps to be opened by the clasped lance-thrust of the mailed fist. Here is indeed the male lily, now spent, fallen and broken in the pass of love. Here is the tensed sperm-head of the lifted organ, leaded in glass and filled with the green seed of leaf and twig. The swell and thrust of Mariana's breast against the side of the organ-shape, the leveling of her mouth as if to kiss its point—these hold and underline the pent message of the confrontation: *I want to, but I can't, because I mustn't.* A sense almost of renunciation seems to come from the shapes of the eager breasts pushed in the air behind her by her arms, and from the tight hold of her girdle on the discreetly purpled buttocks too voluptuously promising in their reminiscence of an Etty nude's. Here the repressed and desperate sexuality of mid-Victorian society is forced hard-on against the gridirons of convention.

Of course, even adverse criticism could be led astray by these. Ruskin could only find the corner toilet-table "idolatrous," and indeed it does mingle the cosmetic with the liturgical. It could be further argued, however, as Ruskin failed to see, that the cosmetic ministers to the girl's vanity are molded as implicit sexual metaphors. The brazier of in-

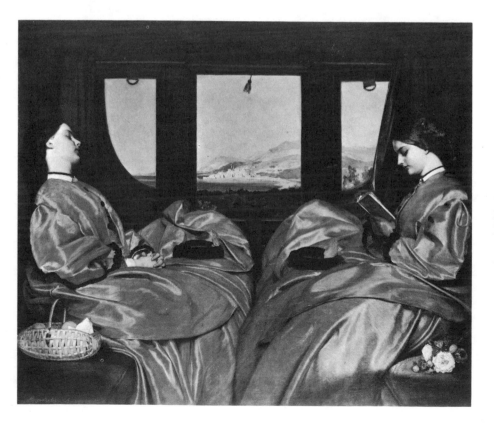

Salvador Dali: *The Persistence of Memory,* 1931, 9 1/2 inches high. Museum of Modern Art, New York.

Augustus Leopold Egg: *The Traveling Companions,* 1862, 25 3/8 inches high. City Museum and Art Gallery, Birmingham

Yves Tanguy: *The Furniture of Time*, 1939, 45 7/8 inches high. Collection James T. Soby, New Canaan, Conn.

James Tissot: *Boarding the Yacht*, 1873, 30 inches high. Collection P. M. Samuel, London.

cense glows in the shape of the *mons Veneris*. It might easily have derived from some medieval chastity-belt imagined for the damned by Brueghel or Bosch. Even the folding triptych can be seen as encouragingly akimbo, in blatant invitation to the hard stance of the phallic nard-sprinkler. Every detail, in fact, serves as a profound buttressing for the religious wounding that Millais is concerned with. One could hardly laugh at a modern prude who found the image too blasphemously erotic. Aroused intellectuals might find it more effective as a masturbatory fantasy than anything from the *Strong Stocking* cabinets of Soho booksellers. One compares its impact with the record-breaking New York poster of a nun adjusting her garter. Tennyson had given his contemporaries a poem about rarefied feelings unrequited. From Millais those who could read it had a painting about acute physical need. The distance between them is the jump from Regency permissiveness to Victorian censorship. One should not be too surprised that the stronger generator of eroticism is the society of repression.

In Henry Wallis' *The Death of Chatterton*, 1856, the art of need can be studied in more detail. We approach an apparently fictive and elevated work, whose real subject is more coarsely autobiographical, urging us into the byways of a steamy early Victorian scandal. The model for the dead poet in the painting was the novelist and verse writer George Meredith. Two years later the artist eloped with Meredith's wife, an episode celebrated in that masterpiece of innovatory sonneteering, *Modern Love*. In the context of this bizarrely poignant history, an informed student will approach the picture as an ironic icon of art's influence on life. Its surface impact as a rather sentimental, not to say glamorizing, image of a prematurely eclipsed genius, killed by a society which misunderstands him (as perhaps Regency England misunderstood Keats, "the marvelous boy") is bound to recede, and become disconnected. Instead, one confronts the powerful compressed sexuality of a work whose primary concern is the exquisite lassitude of gratified desire. The shape of the man's body is that of an unstrung bow, limp and yet supple as

33

Dante Gabriel Rossetti:
*The Girlhood of Mary
Virgin,* 1849, detail,
32 3/4 inches high.
Tate Gallery, London.

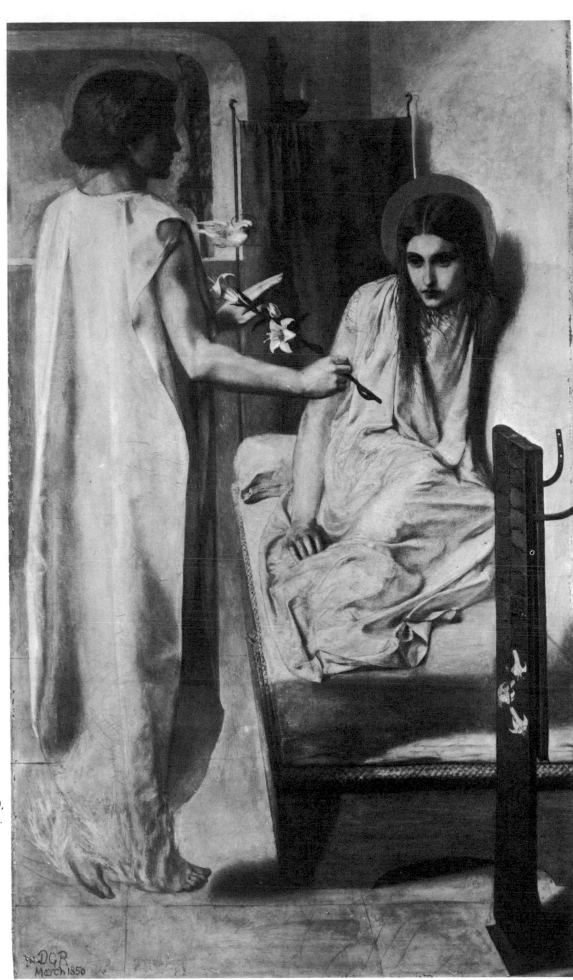

Rossetti's *Ecce Ancilla Domini (The Annunciation)*, 1850, 28 1/2 inches high. Tate Gallery, London.

Richard Dadd: *The Fairy Feller's Master Stroke,* 1855-64,
21 1/4 inches high. Tate Gallery, London.

Hugo Simberg: *Death and the Peasant*, 1896, tempera, 24 1/2 inches high. The Ateneum Art Museum, Helsinki.

Henry Wallis: *The Death of Chatterton*, 1856,
23 3/4 inches high. Tate Gallery, London.

the length of a sinewy cat stretched before a fire. For the moment the body's seed is spent and scattered, as the torn paper on the attic floor, but there is still a rich store contained in the provokingly open box, and the sculptured folds of the breeches in the man's groin promise a forthcoming return of mustered energy. At the poet's head the tensed folds of his pillow knot in the rough shape of a nipple, perhaps one strained in nylon or kinky leather by an artist such as Oldenburg or Christo. On the right of the picture, the snuffed candle is no longer an image for death (as in Shakespeare's, though not perhaps in Fuseli's, *Macbeth*) but a more piquantly Freudian indicator of remaindered potency. In this light, the poet's body begins to assume a more sensuous outline—perhaps that of a deliciously erogenous banana, or (to the alertly Surreal eye) the exhausted fish-woman in Magritte's *L'Invention Collective.* The painting is finally one of laxness, of rest. As an image of death, it dwindles in power, too hopeful of an innocent resurrection. The poet looks as if he is only sleeping. Read, however, as a picture of a beautiful youth at rest—with a secondary suggestion of the little death in sex—it takes on a more stealthy and fertile energy, framed and

given body by the true life story it mirrors, conceals, and obliquely comments on.

In Richard Dadd's compact oil *The Fairy Feller's Master-Stroke*, painted between 1855 and 1864, the notion of two levels, or layers, of interpretation is given a physical presence by the external structure of the image. At the same time, the autobiographical element very efficiently masters, and controls, the fictive one. In the foreground we seem to crouch behind, and peer through, rather than approach, a densely myopic screen of interlacing and interwoven grasses, which cover the surface area of the small canvas in a manner convincing us of our inferior size. These huge diagonals are inevitably grass, and yet indubitably larger than we are as we edge through them. On the ground behind their screen, reminiscent to the Abstract-Expressionist eye of the shallow space created by the slash and drip flow of a Pollock, a macabre nightmare is being enacted. A group of dwarfish and misshapen figures is dispersed across a rocky hillside where a large-headed alarmed old man is crouched facing forward with his hands on his knees. A powerful younger man stands with his back to us, raising a heavy mallet with

38

which he may be about to crack open a glossy-looking sweet chestnut. I say "may" be, since the expression of the old man, and the alignment of the mallet, leave open the alternative interpretation that the blow is aimed at his bald and exposed skull. Anyone familiar with the gruesome story of how the painter murdered his father, and was later incarcerated in the Hospital of St. Mary of Bethlehem suffering from acute schizophrenia, is unlikely to rule out the possibility that the painting may be a nine-year meditation on, or abreaction of, this incident. Significantly enough, one of the few figures in the painting whose face we do not see is the young man with the mallet. He remains focused to a brutal gesture, as menacing and anonymous as the *Doppelgänger* in the empty mirror. All that we know of him are the products of his visceral imagination, the distorted and unkempt ephemera of the subconscious mind, thrown up and evacuated as fairy detritus across the blank hind wall of the picture's world. For these terrible phantoms there is no way out, penned on one side by the ground scattered with nuts and leaves, on the other side by the lashing greens of the laced grasses. As surely as in a prison or an asylum, the mind feeds on its own horrors. What might once have seemed no more than a witty romp with trolls

and pixies, albeit with a grotesquely puzzling resonance, takes on through the context of biography the shudder of a notebook entry from bedlam.

This element of a madhouse realism recurs frequently in the work of a Finnish painter of the '90s, Hugo Simberg, whose compressed and skeletal imagination cracks open the frail skin of the legends he overtly deals with. With him, however, as with his countryman, Akseli Gallén-Kallela, in his more dream-like moods, the characteristically British divergence between the ostensible and the real subjects of the paintings is less apparent. The terror, and its resonance, is nearer the surface, though for this reason perhaps ultimately less trenchant and fearsome.

It remains, perhaps, to argue for the intention behind this cryptic *trompe-l'esprit*. I suspect, as the analogy of Victorian poetry supports, that the *mores* of post-Regency society inevitably restricted the kind of uninhibited treatment of sex and violence open to an artist such as Fuseli or Byron. Art had to go underground, as surely as piano legs had to go into frilly knickers. What merits our attention is the view that a prudish need for such disguise is the most emphatic indicator of an intense, productive, eventually satisfying involvement.

René Magritte: *The Collective Invention,* 1934,
31 7/8 inches high. Collection E.L.T. Mesens, London.

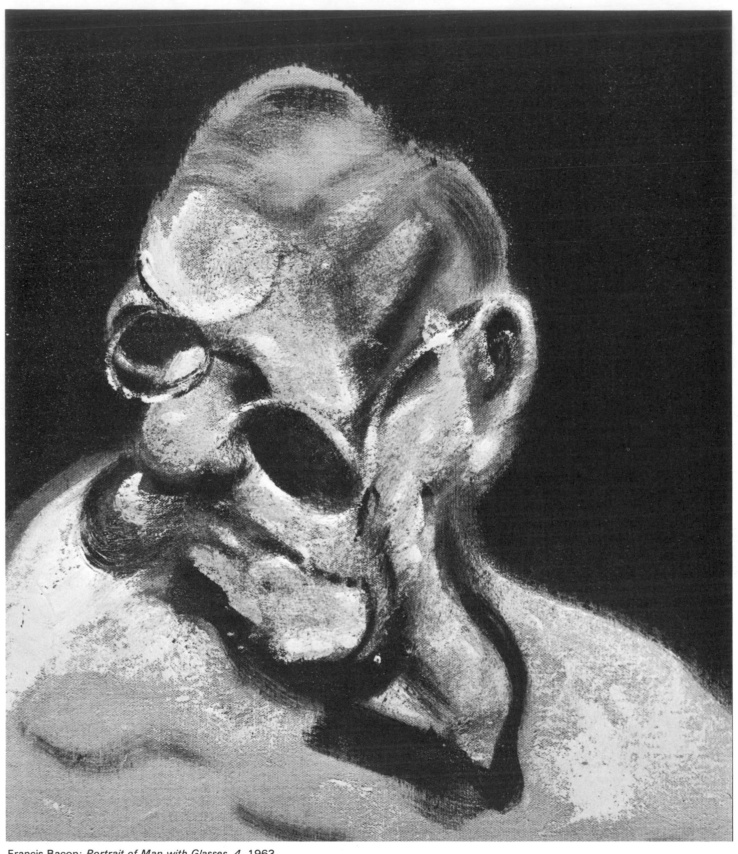

Francis Bacon; *Portrait of Man with Glasses, 4,* 1963,
13½ inches high. Private collection, London.

By Fairfield Porter

Speaking Likeness

**In its emphasis on particularity, on the individual
sitter as well as on the individual work,
portraiture reveals the weakness of modern art dogma**

A good work of art can in its entirety be represented only by itself.
Tolstoy

Figure painting and especially portraiture contradict twentieth-century esthetic dogma. Alex Katz said that when you paint a portrait the difficulty is that you have to get a likeness *and* make the paint go across the canvas. This implies a paradoxical combination: that there is nothing of art in the first necessity, and nothing but art in the second. I intend to argue that there is no paradox, and that to think that there is, is to misunderstand all art.

In the nineteenth century it was commonly believed that truth in art meant "likeness" to objective nature. In Eakins' time science was empirical, and Eakins placed his trust in an assumed projection from the object through the lens of his eye to the canvas. Art was projective geometry. The Impressionists relied more simply on seeing itself, without reference to what it might be that they saw. Seurat had to verify seeing by routing it through his conscious mind, as Stravinsky says he has to do with his muscular activities in order to be able to walk, now that he has reached the age of 86. In the nineteenth century, science was empirical, but the empirical element is being continually reduced in modern science. The ultimate realities of physics are expressed mathematically, which is to say in ideal terms.

Twentieth-century esthetics comes from the reaction against Impressionism and is supported by the tendency of modern science to grow away from empirical fact and reduce the totality of everything that exists to essential and manipulable ideas. Twenty years ago in the conversations of those painters around whose talks the Eighth Street Club was formed, it was common to disparage "illusion." The illusory is

Author: Fairfield Porter, one of the best-known American realists, recently had a major retrospective at the Cleveland Museum; last year he was visiting professor at Amherst.

what probably does not exist, you can see it as you see a ghost. It may be a trick, a deceit. What is real enough to place your confidence in? If it is form, what is form in visual art? Is it order? Is it something which makes sense? Is what makes sense an essence that can be extracted from the thing? Is it a translation—an expression in other terms? There is a school of criticism that seems to take off from semantics, that tries for scientific objectivity, and is connected with art education in colleges and universities. What one can make sense of, to talk about, must be presented logically, following the rules of language. I think this criticism derives from the enormous prestige of science consequent on its useful applications. Science looms over us; it dominates education; and according to what an increasing number of scientists increasingly say, in its practical applications it threatens within a generation or a century to make the planet uninhabitable for all vertebrates, bees and flowering plants. The threat is both enhanced and hastened by technological solutions. As Barry Commoner said at an anti-pollution meeting in London last fall, there is something basically wrong with technology.

What is wrong is that the scientific notion of reality, which is at the bottom of technology, is inadequate. It is inadequate because it is limited by the idealism of the scientific method. The practical successes of science come from a reduction of the totality of "everything that is the case" to what can be used. Science uses facts as though they were the replaceable parts of a mass-produced machine: what counts is their similarity, their replaceability: that which recurs. The uniformity of nature is a scientific ultimate within which all events take place and towards which all processes return. This view of reality ignores the specific quality of facts, which are notoriously arbitrary.

The scientist does not go as far in the direction of ideality as the mathematician. The mathematician's facts, having no material existence, can be manipulated with absolute certainty. Science does not deal with absolute certainties, and a general-

Lucian Freud: *Head of a Girl,*
tempera. Private collection, London.

Alberto Giacometti: *Portrait of Annette,* 1957,
28 3/8 inches high. Kunsthaus, Zurich.

Edouard Vuillard: *Mme. Gillou at Home*, 1931, 28½ inches high. The man
standing is the composer-pianist Reynaldo Hahn. Knoedler, New York.

Bonnard's portrait of his dealers, J. and G. Bernheim-Jeune,
1920, 65 inches high. Musée d'Art Moderne, Paris.

Degas: *The Duke and Duchess of Morbilli*. 1867, 45 5/8 inches
high. The Duchess was Thérèsè, the artist's sister. Boston Museum

ization from material facts can only be an approximation, and manipulations of these approximations can therefore lead only to approximate results. What in science is called proof is not absolute as in mathematics, but rather a demonstration of a very high degree of likelihood: it is assumed that what seems most likely to happen, will happen. Yet the connection with the particular and the arbitrary grows more and more tenuous. That modern science leaves experience ever farther behind is attested by Buckminster Fuller's reply to the (naturally hypothetical) question, "where do you live?" with the proud banality that he lives on Spaceship Earth; and to the question who he is, with the equally proud and apathetic reply that he does not know. These questions, he seems to indicate, have no scientific significance, which to a layman is like saying that they do not exist.

When Bertrand Russell investigated the question of knowledge, he found that he could reduce knowledge to three principles, and from these principles build up again, first mathematics, next physics, then chemistry, presumably followed by biology. These principles come out of the theory of numbers, so they establish a mathematical basis for truth. They are: quantity, class and the idea of the successor. But

he could not derive from these principles an explanation for the way in which the weather never exactly repeats itself. He could not derive from them the fact of communication, that even creatures of different zoological orders, as for instance a dog and a porpoise, understand each other somewhat, without translation into some mediating logical system. The quality of communication is not illuminated by explanation: nevertheless it exists.

Art critics who have been impressed by positivism want their criticism to make sense in the way that Russell's logic does: they have the layman's disbelief in the existence of that which is without scientific significance. As in science, what has significance in this esthetic are events that recur, and recurrence is artistic form, which it is possible to talk about only insofar as it is logical, and can be translated or measured. This measure is its validity; it is what can be taught. The most formal is the most general, the most amenable to systematic translation. Wittgenstein had the idea that to know an event as one knows a proposition in logic, it is necessary to translate it into a picture of itself, according to rules of logic. In a way this is the reverse of the verification of art by criticism, for it implies the use of art to know nature. The picture reinforces

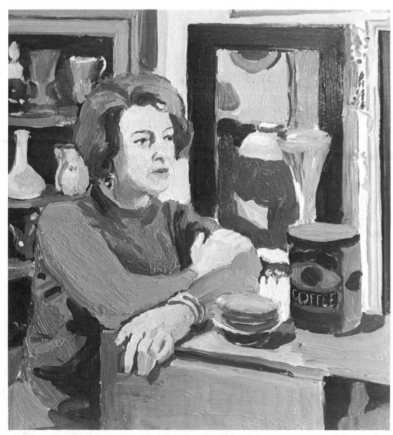

Fairfield Porter: *Portrait of Inez MacWhinnie*, 1968, 20 inches high. Collection of the artist.

Larry Rivers: *Portrait of Joseph H. Hirshhorn*, 1963, 71 inches high. Hirshhorn Collection, New York.

one's belief in the reality of the existence of the facts to which an experience refers. What good is art if it has no connection with the truth, and what better way is there than the logical way of getting hold of the truth?

Logic is a criticism of experience. The ability to communicate implies the ability to manipulate, which is most complete when, as in mathematics, the terms of the communication are reduced to immateriality or the ideal; for in the material world one comes up against the intractability of fact. Since a fact is specific, as part of a generalization it will lose specificity: its integrity will be destroyed.

A scientific proposition which has to keep the connection with material fact requires, to persuade one of its truth, the assumption that what is almost certain (almost capable of truth) is true enough. It follows that a scientific proposition is almost communicable. But when one's concern is, like an artist's, with the arbitrary and the particular, there can be no "logical" communication at all, for the arbitrariness of the

original experience will not survive a generalization that is necessary for logical communication. The question comes up, has the arbitrary got form? Is it real? Material form is always arbitrary, and cannot be expressed by essence or elixir, and to know the arbitrary exactly is to know something that cannot be generalized. Wittgenstein came apparently to believe this, as indicated in his remark that "every sentence is in order as it is." The form of the arbitrary, the order of the material world of fact that is there as it stands, being insusceptible to depiction by logic, cannot be part of the world of either mathematics or science. It is a world in which what is certain cannot be repeated. I believe this is the world of art.

Art connects us with the material world, from which mathematics, science and technology separate us. It is concerned with the particular; it reconciles us to the arbitrary. Artistic particularity has no connection with technological generality. The concern of technology is to even out, to bring about that uniformity of nature envisaged by the idealism re-

Alex Katz: *Portrait of Elaine de Kooning*, 1965, 22 inches high. Collection Harold Brown.

Elaine de Kooning: *Portrait of Conrad,* 1955,
40 inches high. Graham Gallery.

Willem de Kooning: *Portrait of Rudolph Burckhardt* (unfinished),
ca. 1939, 48 inches high. Collection Edwin Denby and R. Burckhardt.

Balthus: *The Vicomtesse de Noailles,* 1936, 62¼ inches high. Collection Vicomte Charles de Noailles, Paris.

Alex Katz: *Purple Series, 1,* 1964,
22 inches high. Fischbach Gallery.

quired by the effective working of its methods. The purpose of technology is, in effect, to hasten the process of entropy—in short, to destroy. Insofar as twentieth-century esthetics derives from the idealism of logical positivism, it serves the purpose of promoting, like technology, our separation from the world of material fact, and it is opposed to art. And so also are those artists allied with technology, such as most architects and industrial designers.

If a good work of art cannot be represented in other terms than itself, how does one talk about it? The answer is, in analogies. A description bears a family resemblance to its subject rather than reproducing it. An intelligent esthetic analysis uses the concepts of quality, relationship and the transition. Being outside of logic, these concepts do not "make sense," and since they are untranslatable they are not "useful." Art discovers a reality that human intelligence is not coextensive with and that cannot be manipulated. One understands material reality by experience. One understands art by imaginative identification, which is also the way the artist (or scientist, or logician) discovers his subject in the first place. Wallace Stevens said the aim of poetry was "without imposing, without reasoning at all, to find the eccentric at the base

of design." This is both the artist's vision and his sense of order.

A good portrait presents this irreducible reality that the artist's vision and sense of order are one. This quality was described by Francis Bacon referring to the Rembrandt self-portrait at Aix, in which the "mystery of fact is conveyed by an image being made out of non-rational marks," and by Giacometti, speaking of his own work: "I worked from the model throughout the day from 1935 to 1940. Nothing was like what I imagined it to be. A head (I soon left the figure aside; it was too much) became an object completely unknown and without dimensions." A portrait by Vuillard presents the fact of the relationship of facts and the unexpectedness of the most ordinary transitions between them. It adds up to a world whose quality, as Claude Roger-Marx more or less put it, is of one in which "the habitual lives in an enchanted domain." The reality discovered by Giacometti is that the minuteness of man marks a beginning for the immensity of space.

If I described in this manner the other portraits illustrating this article, it would weaken my point that to understand art is to make an imaginative identification with it. It is already enough to have chosen examples.

Alice Neel: *Portrait of Edward Avedisian,* 1961, 50 inches high. Collection of the artist.

Jane Freilicher: *Self-Portrait,* 1963, 40 inches high. Collection Stratford College, Stratford, Conn.

Saul Steinberg: *Geography*, 1964, 29 inches high.

By John Ashbery

Saul Steinberg: Callibiography

**His life, from Wunderkind in Bucharest to celebrity on the
New York-Paris-Milan exhibition axis, is told in
drawings which, as he has remarked, are 'a form of writing'**

When Saul Steinberg met Henry Moore last year, the latter happened to mention that he had decided to be a sculptor at the age of 12. "I was unable to tell him at what point I decided to become an artist," Steinberg recalled recently, "because I never decided and I still have not done so." After allowing a pause to accumulate he added, "I decided to become a novelist when I was 10. I prepared my life in terms of causing the sort of actions that would make me a novelist. But then I became something else."

Steinberg made these remarks in a suitably novelistic setting, the living room of his house at The Springs, the artists' colony near East Hampton, Long Island where he spends his summers. It's a little old shingled house which he says looks like "a Chaplin dream of happiness." D. W. Griffith would no doubt have felt at home in it too, and the front screen door seems to be waiting for Mary Pickford to fling it open and rush ecstatically down the steps, all curls to the wind. One thinks too of the novels of Gene Stratton Porter and Harold Bell Wright from which these old flicks were made, or at least of the perfectly accurate idea one has of them without ever having read them, just as one need not try to decipher the insane calligraphy in a Steinberg official document to guess its import. The furnishings of this fictional bungalow were found by Steinberg, but they look as though he designed them: their shapes are eccentric but crisp and somehow definitive. A Tiffany-style lampshade over the dining-room table has an insistent design like ribbon candy. Underneath it is a platter with an unusually clean-cut example of the blue willow pattern, with which Steinberg apparently has a love-hate relationship. Two carefully chosen specimens of Art Deco furniture copy the vehemence of Steinberg's line, and suggest that rectilinearity had been achieved only after a struggle.

The role that narrative plays in Steinberg's art is a crucial but acentral one. For a hundred years painters have cringed at the idea of "telling a story," and it is only recently that we have been able again to appreciate pictures like the Victorian ones discussed elsewhere in this volume. Except for Expressionism the major movements in the art of our century, from the Fauves to the Minimalists, have shared the premise that art is something uniquely visual, an idea that to me seems as far-fetched as the currently accepted notion that poetry should use as few adjectives as possible, presumably because description belongs to the domain of the visual arts. But why shouldn't painting tell a story, or not tell one, as it sees fit? Why should poetry be intellectual and non-sensory, or the reverse? Our eyes, minds and feelings do not exist in isolated compartments but are part of each other, constantly cross-cutting, consulting and reinforcing each other. An art constructed according to the above canons, or any others, will wither away since, having left one or more of the faculties out of account, it will eventually lose the attention of the others.

But for Steinberg, whose wit and success have delayed his recognition as a serious artist, the case must present itself somewhat differently. For this frustrated novelist turned draftsman, "art" is something that gets in the way of narration, impeding it and finally, as though by accident, enriching it to the point where it becomes something else—the history of its own realized and unrealized potentialities, a chronicle of used time on a level with Giacometti's histories of his hesitations or Pollock's diaries of change. The finished product is an ambiguously whole record of experience, a verbal proposition that puts up with the laws of visual communication merely so as to confound them more thoroughly. The message of a Steinberg picture is therefore offstage, but for it to exist the stage has to be set.

This is Steinberg's situation. It is the reason why he has adapted the form of the cartoon to his own purposes. The drawings are not cartoons, but they produce the same reflex —one looks, thinks and reaches a decision. It is an art that appeals to the intellect through the senses. And it is doubt-

1943, 1965, 14½ inches high.

Biography, 1968, 32 inches high.

less the only kind of art that an artist of such peculiar refinement as Steinberg would produce. He is interested, he says, in understanding—the last of the three stages (sensation and perception being the first two) by which we are classically supposed to acquire knowledge.

"The bourgeoisie is happy with perceptions. They see a Vasarely, their eyeballs twitch and they're happy. I am concerned with the memory, the intellect, and I do not wish to stop at perception. Perception is to art what one brick is to architecture." And he went on to elaborate by telling about a disappointing childhood experience. The boy next door was the son of a contractor, and one day there was a large pile of bricks in the yard. His friend told Saul that the next day they would make a house. He spent a sleepless night anticipating this adventure, and the next day found that his friend had already begun work on the house—which, with a rusty nail, he was carving out of a single brick.

The information-gathering character of all of Steinberg's work becomes almost a paroxysm in certain instances—notably his now widely-imitated abstract comic strips, where lines, shapes, blips and unintelligible words are the vectors of a seemingly precise message; and in the rebus-like drawings he has done recently. One of these consists of a sort of chorus-line of radical signs ($\sqrt{\ }$) facing an array of question marks. The "message" is: "Radicals Question Marx." Yet the pursuit of understanding continues throughout his oeuvre, even at its sweetest and most sensuous-seeming, such as a drawing called *Autobiography* which presents elements from his childhood (a sexy lady in a park, his father's shop, a trolley lettered "Westinghouse"—it seems they had Westinghouse trolleys in Bucharest in the 'twenties) in a Proustian ambiance of juvenile eroticism. The line refers the image to the brain by the directest route.

Prompted by my interest in *Autobiography* to speak again of his early ambition to be a novelist, Steinberg added: "Rumania is a perfect place for a novelist, because you're not protected. At five or ten you already have a full knowledge of human nature. You didn't have to be told the facts of life, you saw brutality, goodness, sex—all the human facets. I have friends who went to school in Lausanne and who will never know about life. Our system of over-protectiveness precludes the development of *Wunderkinder.* It's impossible

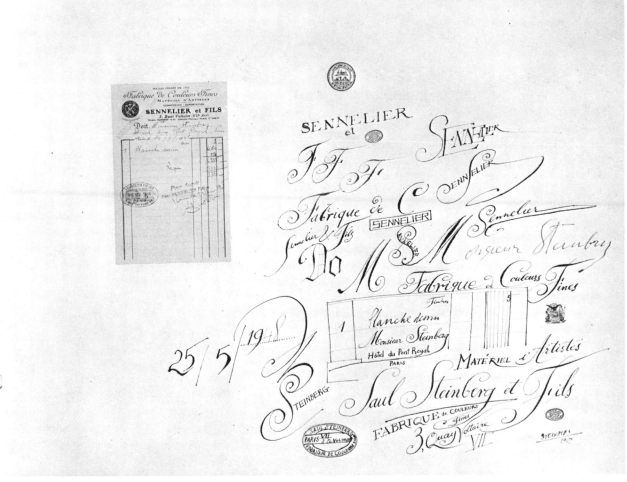

Sennelier, 1967, 22½ inches high.

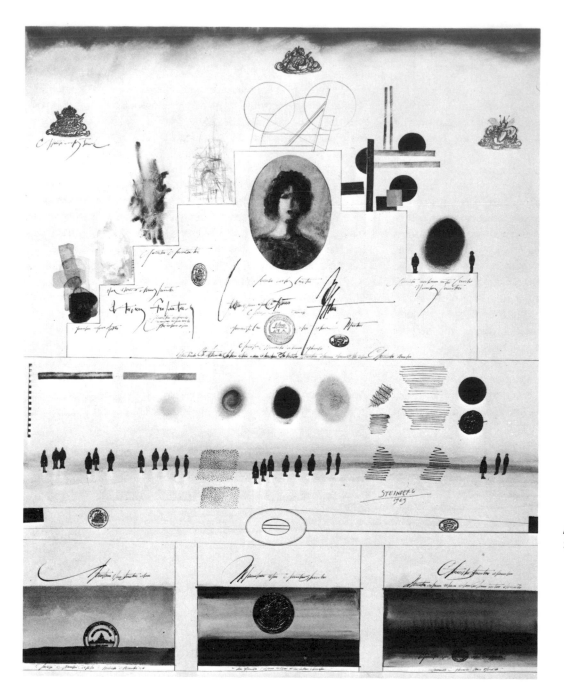

Biography, 1968
32 inches high.

to become an intellectual if you haven't been a *Wunderkind.* What you learn from books and meditation is much less important than what you learn fresh from the egg." With such a philosophy, it is not surprising that Steinberg turned into what he is: an artist animated by an amiable, if difficult, directness.

The directness has been honed by the discipline of producing for an upper-middlebrow mass medium like *The New Yorker.* Steinberg considers the *New Yorker* drawings as separate from his other work. He calls them "homework" and "calisthenics," since "everything has to be understood at once. I have built a muscle through homework, so that everything else is child's play. So did Seurat, who thought of himself as a scientist. What is great in him is his vision, but technique was his camouflage. I believe in Eliot's advice to poets: Do something else. Left to your own devices you get fat and start slumming. In the Renaissance artists were workers—

builders and constructors had their say, and the artist was part of a team. Since the Impressionists (except for Seurat), art has become no homework.

"The New Yorker is my 'political' world. My duty. I am formulating a subversive political message. My other drawings are political only in the sense that I am concerned with autobiography. I mind my own business, talk about myself. When I make a drawing for myself I use only my pleasure."

At the moment his pleasure consists in re-conjugating the themes that have always preoccupied him: time, space, history, geography, biography. They are always emerging in new and amusing ways, but together they form the fixed center of his work: a kind of organ point, something too wry to be called nostalgia but certainly close to it—perhaps the effort of a wry mind to come to terms with its nostalgia. And so we have "biographies" like the one of Millet, an artist whom

56

Il Gabinetto del Proprio Niente,
1965, 29 inches high.

Steinberg likes because he was born exactly one century before him, in 1814, and because "he tried to combine Raphael with socialism." (Currently Steinberg is fascinated by the two figures in *The Angelus*, and has had a rubber stamp made of them so he can place them in all sorts of unaccustomed environments, such as the beach at East Hampton or the desert at Gizeh.) The biographies are actually certificates, certifying life by means of official seals and rubber stamps, portrait medallions and passages of handwriting that is illegible but looks as though it ought to be legible ("Biography gets confused with calligraphy. One's life is a form of calligraphy— blunt, brush etc."). And the biographies are related to history, especially art history which he is always mercilessly codifying: "The history of art history is based on the government taking over art and making a political avant-garde *de choc.*" One *Biography* illustrates the various stages in the life of an artist. A tiny, Giacometti-like figure is seen progressing from a sort of monumental pre-existence resembling a Bayreuth set to "cliché reality" or "vernacular reality"—a picturesque little cabin somewhat suggestive of Steinberg's own house, and in fact he explains that "the vernacular is the street you were born in. Once you get out of it you are into 'political' or 'hearsay' reality," which is represented in the drawing by a balloon filled with unintelligible scribblings and a somewhat utopian landscape with a rainbow. This leads to abstract reality, which comes when a man has decided on his principles and which is indicated by clusters of concentric circles. From here one may proceed either to a labyrinth ("total confusion"), to a sort of coat-of-arms ("power and glory—another *cul de sac*") or to a spiral ("a beautiful symbol"). Down below, the same figure is pictured seated at an easel painting the spiral, suggesting both that he has found the true way and that the process, having crystallized back into geometry, is about to begin all over again.

So time is continually cropping out, organizing space and biography according to its cruel whims. In one drawing a figure of a cat is marching down a slope, followed by what looks like a millstone inscribed with a calendar: the cat must keep moving or be crushed by time. Or, again, Steinberg imagines an autobiographical map with the names of all the places where he has spent time neatly lettered and situated by dots with no regard, of course, for geographical reality: Amagansett is lettered much larger than Edinburgh; Mantova, Malaga and Odessa are close together; Milano is situated all alone on an island in a lake on whose shores are London and Paris; and throughout the country meanders the river (of life), its banks dotted with picturesque ports like Laramie, Roma, Anchorage, New York; Leadville, Gallup, Wellfleet and Rochester. Or a moment will be preserved with ironical care: a 1948 receipt from the Paris art supplier Sennelier et Fils is glued to a sheet of drawing paper and its contents copied in Steinberg's painstaking hand, yet despite all the precautions Sennelier et Fils finally becomes Steinberg et Fils, showing how hard it is for the outside world not to recast itself in one's own image. Or autobiography is seen through the refracting lens of art history as in *Steinberg Self-Portrait,* which he calls a "cubisterie"—his own name is given the treatment the Cubists used on words like "Byrrh" and "Le Journal." Or

the ever-recurring blue willow landscape is invaded by foreign autobiographical incrustations such as Long Island saltboxes, a factory and a duomo from a primitive Italian painting. Or one's life is seen as an allegorical "cabinet" in *Il Gabinetto del Proprio Niente*—an alchemist's study furnished with such objects as a huge letter "S," a drafting triangle whose three sides are inscribed "Oh," "Hm" and "Bah," and a chest whose drawers are labeled, "Crime, Punishment, Rouge, Noir, War, Peace, Bouvard, Pécuchet, Pride, Prejudice, Fear, Trembling" —the furniture of life, in Steinberg's phrase.

This last is for me one of Steinberg's most moving drawings, and perhaps epitomizes his strange, comfortably uncomfortable world. Life is a room, empty except for the furniture (no person can enter it because it is already inside us). The furniture is both useful and ornamental, but none of it will be used because no one will ever descend the steps marked with the days of the week or enter through the open door, beyond which one glimpses a tree whose trunk and branches are marked with inscriptions, too far away, alas, to be readable. Yet it all does have a function, that of a symbol, the only function we need concern ourselves with, since it includes everything by telling about it. The act of story-telling alone is of any consequence; what is said gets said anyway, and manner is the only possible conjugation of matter. Or, in Robert Graves's terse summation: "There is one story and one story only."

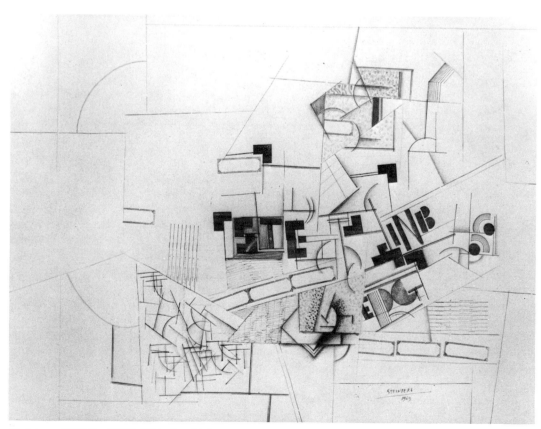

Steinberg Still-Life, 1969, 23 inches high.

La Vie de Millet, 1969, oil on canvas, 24 inches high

Cairo 1943, 1967, 23 inches high.

Mel Bochner: *Language Is Not Transparent,* 1970, 77 inches high, paint and chalk applied
to the wall of the Dwan Gallery, New York during its "Language" show, June, 1970.

By Amy Goldin

Words in Pictures

**In modern art, words and pictures are not separate realms,
but are treated as comparable outcroppings of the
human condition, as equal and as unequal as nails and hair**

What language does art speak? In England the Parliament buildings speak Gothic. In Washington, D.C., the Capitol, banks and post offices all speak Greek. Gauguin's holy mother presumably speaks Tahitian and church Latin. Despite all this, visual art is supposedly non-verbal and talks in the tongue of angels. But is art addressed to angels?

Theoretically, visual imagery is universal. It is supposed to transcend local dialects, making words alien to it or, at best, merely decorative—borrowed plumage. Stern estheticians claim that because language arts are temporal while visual arts are spatial, they should be kept as separate realms with strict extradition treaties between them. Indeed, artistic mixtures of verbal and visual elements are felt to be transcendentally unkosher, or at least esthetically déclassé. Nor is this prejudice limited to art theory. It is brought forward again and again in practical criticism. When the movies became the talkies, the art of the film was supposed to go into a decline. Talking about art is supposed to blight creativity. Conceptual art's intense involvement with language suggests that its visibility is trivial.

In fact, however, the visual arts are saturated with language, and our artistic experiences are generally dominated by it. This is especially true of experts. Lessing wrote about expression and the Laocoön without ever having seen the original marble. His theory was based on engravings—and words. The idea that art imitates nature is a verbal idea. There is no such thing as subject matter in nature. Subject matter is a category of intellectual history. Without words and labels you don't know what you're looking at. As clothes make the man, language makes the picture. With pictures and people,

Author: Amy Goldin has contributed a number of essays on recent developments in Concept Art to *Art News;* last winter she taught at the University of California in San Diego.

our knowledge is based on names and the conventions of public performance.

Is the painted lady a saint? A queen? A courtesan? Or not a lady at all? Greece on the ruins of Missolonghi, perhaps, or Liberty leading the people? Or one of that horde of traveling female abstractions that poets continually were trying to banish or invoke? We read "Hence, loathed Melancholy..." or "Inoculation, heavenly maid, descend..." to the accompaniment of fluttering draperies. We recognize the art game by reading the names of the players.

To deny the relevance of language to art is to make the astounding assumption that stylistic and iconographic conventions are self-explanatory. Presumably, people of taste are artistically literate at birth. Since the decorum of modern esthetics decrees that only color and form REALLY count, it is gauche to look at anything else. Indifference to labels when looking at pictures becomes a mark of basic esthetic competence, like not moving your lips when you read. Yet as bare visual experience, contemporary art is about as readily communicative as moon rocks.

Even when we try to abstract ourselves from all extravisual concerns, however, our response to form draws on body feelings which are modified by cultural norms. Things like the physical constriction we feel from a crowded, bustling canvas or the emotional energy we sense from a pure, high-keyed palette are affected by the way specific cultures value and define privacy or intimacy, expressiveness or restraint. Here I want to insist that when we register the presence or absence of identifiable imagery we are involved in learned responses and specific concepts. The "free" associations we make to art are not personal, but are matters of deliberate artistic control. Artistic meaning is characteristically overdetermined—that is, many causes operate to achieve something we experience as a simple, unified effect. Words are visible and their role is less trivial than we suspect, but the buried force of language as the repository of general notions

Théodore Géricault: *The Raft of the Medusa,*
1818-19, 158 inches high. Louvre, Paris.

These pictures embody a variety of word-image relationships
usually lumped together as symbolism. Yet we call the
Cole an "allegory," the Delacroix "illustration" and the
Géricault "documentation." Homer, with his title, rejects
human reference in favor of geography. Lorenz Eitner has
discussed the storm-tossed boat as a major image in
Romantic iconography, a reference to human vulnerability
and forces beyond human control. How do we know that this
idea-image is irrelevant to Christ on the Sea of Galilee?

Christ on the Sea of Galilee, from the Gospels of
Abbess Hitda of Meschede, Cologne, 11th century.

Eugène Delacroix: *Dante and Virgil in the Inferno,*
1822, 74 inches high. Louvre, Paris.

Thomas Cole: *The Voyage of Life: Manhood,* 1840, 52 inches
high. Munson-Williams-Proctor Institute, Utica. N.Y.

is enormous. The importance of art's cultural context is universally acknowledged, which means that nobody thinks about it. But who can think about anything so murky? And how could the phrase be unraveled, except to point at such things as site, function and language?

The acute dependency of pictures on language is fundamentally linked to the mobility of easel painting. When art is physically inseparable from its setting, it is on that account better equipped to hold onto its meanings. At Susa the Lion Gates said something like this: "We guard the precincts of a powerful king, and our permanence, our discipline, our gorgeousness are his." The message was delivered first by the setting, and only secondly by the architectural medium, the subject matter, and esthetic properties of shape, color and pattern. As long as the Lion Gates remained on the site they made sense. The concepts of the sacred precinct and of imperial power remained alive long after the last Assyrian had forgotten the Sumerian word for eggs. The conceptual language of the gates was embedded in their site, size and presentational form—in their function as boundaries and barriers.

Documents, however, are rootless and—relatively—mute. Documents are vague because they are unbound to the situation to which they refer. A document is, above all, a set of internal relations, and it must be located in a wider context before it makes sense as a whole. Documents need words. Turned into a photograph in a book or a fragment in a museum, the Lion Gates become documents. As documents, they whisper while the label and catalogue number speak, telling us provenance, date, size, material. If we are literate, patient and diligent, some vague idea of the gates can be reconstituted from this accumulation of information. A chunk of the original gate tells the uninitiated precisely nothing.

The setting, the physical and social site of experience, is the first determinant of artistic meaning. Cultural loot, art dispossessed of its place in the human fabric, segregated in museums and turned into documents of art history, is art that needs somehow to be relocated in a human context. Consequently, the need for language. And what we largely know as art *is* cultural loot. Since displaced objects always need extensive verbal operations before they can be coaxed into resuming communication with us, museum art is word business, a matter for scholarship and talk. The idea of a purely expressive art, independent of local considerations or language, is a myth.

The mutual entanglement of concepts and images has always been a source of the power of art. With conceptual art that secret is now in the open. The fallacy of the purely visual sense-datum—the basis of formalist esthetics—is exposed. Seeing is not sensation with interpretation added. All seeing is dominated by aspect, that is to say, by the viewer's interests and the presentational context in which visual encounters take place. No eye is innocent. What we see depends on how and why we are looking, and we do not ever simply reflect the contents of the visual field. Seeing is not a mechanical act. It is a complexly determined relationship in which habitual expectations and ideas play a major role.

Only when language enters the visual field as print, however, has the relevance of language to art been officially inescapable.

In the West, words first appeared in pictures as labels. Sometimes images were differentiated *only* by print, as, for example, in early book illustrations where a single townscape served for any city by being labeled "Rome" or "Jerusalem" or "Antioch." Here words lend specificity.

On the other hand, mottos, emblematic letters or phrases associated with a depicted figure tend to move the spectator's attention in the opposite direction, away from the appearance of an individualized image and toward the more general idea that was to be associated with it. Sometimes this general idea could be presented as direct speech. The

Winslow Homer: *The Gulf Stream,* 1899, 28 1/8 inches high. Metropolitan Museum, New York

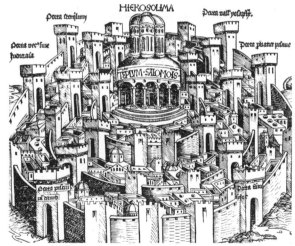

Image identifiable only through its title: generalized medieval cityscape is labeled *Jerusalem* (Chronicle of Hartmann-Schedel).

figure "addressed" the viewer in print suspended in pictorial space or coming out of his mouth, comic-book fashion. Like all the uses of print we have mentioned so far, there is no significant tension here between pictorial and verbal syntax. Either can be taken as an illustration of the other. The words are meant to be read and print serves primarily to reduce uncertainty about pictorial meaning by increasing redundancy.

This is not the case when we encounter print in twentieth-century paintings. Here words are less referential than associative, an observation of the ubiquitous presence of advertising and mass communication in urban life. Words like "Journal" in a Cubist collage, or GAS, EAT, STOP in a Stuart Davis are not messages but capitalism and technology expressing themselves. Typography and signs are not just reading material but contemporary landscape.

Understanding the *role* of words—visible language—is usually more important than being able to read what the words mean. The difference between a saint's name in a Byzantine mosaic and *"Ma Jolie"* in a Picasso is least of all a difference in the meaning of the words. What we need to know for artistic purposes is that words are likely to be labels in the first case and motifs in the second. Once we have learned the clues that identify differences in function, words in pictures are never wholly unintelligible, even when they're in languages we can't read.

The main clue to the function of words in pictures is position. Words in central and off-axis positions, especially if they are active in the play of pictorial rhythms and forms, will be motifs. Labels for individual parts tend to halo or abut the forms they identify. Titles—labels for the entire image—are set out of the way, conventionally at the bottom of the picture. They "read" as relating to physical, rather than pictorial space. Artist's names can be integrated into the picture-world and insinuated into design, as in David's *Marat* or Ingres' calling-card in *Mme. de Sennones.* But labels and mottos regularly retain a separate identity.

It is a mistake, I think, to distinguish too nicely between words in or under images. It is not a question of how deeply words are embedded in a picture—whether they are locked into pictorial space, lie on the surface or slip off that surface to land on the picture frame or wall. In pictures, words tell us more than what they mean—they become a part of the pictorial grammar. Through their meaning they clue us into the appropriate relations we should take to the image. They guide us to the proper level of abstraction or decorum. They inform us of the artist's conceptual intentions, so that we can recognize the image in terms of its private individuality or its public role. Once we have learned that this is a political figure or a spiritual one, a personality or a social emblem, we identify non-verbal information in terms of its reinforcement or counterpoint to what we read.

Titles are a major device for specifying the rules or terms of our encounter with a work, so that what is visible can be turned into something fully apprehended. They are verbal directions for seeing, context-determining rules for under-

"Words less referential than associative": Gris' *Breakfast,* 1914, 31 7/8 inches high. Museum of Modern Art.

"Understanding the role of words is usually more important than being able to read what they mean": *St. John between St. George and St. Blaise,* 13th century, Novgorod School (42½ inches high; Historical Museum, Moscow) and Picasso's *Ma Jolie,* 1911-12 (39 3/8 inches high; Museum of Modern Art, New York).

Robert Morris: *Swift Night Ruler,* 1963, mixed mediums,
28½ inches wide. Castelli Gallery, New York.

Edward Ruscha: *Cut,* 1969,
36 inches high. Iolas Gallery, New York.

standing. Normally, pictures also contain a wealth of supplementary clues, so that those directions can be ignored as redundant, but they are seldom irrelevant or merely book-keeping devices. Titles can be left unread only when we have already "read" conceptual content from other visual clues. Thus crucifixions can go unlabeled or untitled because nobody in the West can see the image of a crucified man without recognizing it as part of a religious story. Words are unnecessary only when we already know them.

The more a picture deviates from a standard type, the more we need titles. Once an artistic convention is established, however, we need only the barest indication that the work is a member of a class. Titles like *Composition in Blue and Yellow* are perfectly satisfactory guides to perception. They direct us to matters of formal concern and locate artistic intention as clearly as the name of a sitter identifies the painting as a portrait.

With quasi-figurative art, words become major clues to esthetic distance. Miro's *Escargot, Femme, Fleur, Etoile* uses words within the canvas, to keep us from losing the star as an image while he fools around with it as a form. Duchamp's punning titles are essential to our visual pleasure in his art. They transform his rather dry inventions into poetic images, sparkling with allusiveness. Thus he is the inversion of Hieronymus Bosch, whose bland titles deny his visual abandonment to fantasy. And, in modern art, painted words also affirm the flatness of pictorial space by defining a surface.

So natural, so persuasive is the interaction between words and images that non-redundancy is hardly palpable. Non-redundancy begins to be felt only under the impact of contradictory information. What do we make of Whistler's *Arrangement in Black and Grey?* Or of Mondrian's *Broadway Boogie-Woogie?* In both cases the title exerts a countervailing pull against something we have learned as a normal response to stylistic convention. Nudged by the title, we "see" that the *Arrangement* is not exactly a portrait of Whistler's mother—

she is too far from us to be assessed as a personality. The title warns us that we should not respond to the formality of the pose, the withdrawal from intimacy and the coolness of the palette as character traits of the sitter. Yet we aren't likely to think of the lady as a frisky, cookie-making type. Our unsolicited interpretations do not disappear. They are merely lowered in value, and withdraw into shadow as private associations. In the case of the Mondrian, a "proper" reading of the title encourages us to seek out visual rhythms, to read the white as interval rather than space, to see the colors as repetitions of musical notes rather than variations of the square. We will focus on discontinuous patterns and sustained continuities rather than, say, on space or the continuity of lines. Encouraged to seek rhythm, we find it, not in the movement of bodies, but in the shifting beat of colors. Broadway...the commercial theater district, crowds, flashing lights? At any rate, urban mechanism drawn into dance, improvisation on conventional themes. Speed and play. These associations are in some sense corroborated by the title. The title does not lessen the abstractness of the picture, but it does help us to see some abstract things rather than others. It becomes unthinkable, for instance, to call it *Diary of a Seducer,* though Gorky's painting is equally abstract.

A title, then, specifies the intellectual context in which the picture makes sense. It can shift our attention so that we reach for pictorial meaning in an extended or narrowed range. The action shifts to another level, however, with Magritte's *Treason of Images* of 1928-29. The picture consists of an image and a statement. The image is that of a pipe, depicted in profile in a commercial-art style on a flat ground, and *"Ceci n'est pas une pipe"* is written beneath it in the area traditionally assigned to titles. The painted words constitute a grammatically complete proposition, and propose an argument rather than a topic for reverie or speculation. Language gets into the artistic act in a radically new and active way. Words are not motifs, nor labels, nor literary references, locating the

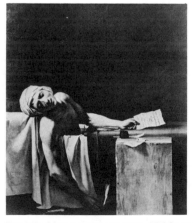

David's *Marat Assassinated,* 1793: the artist makes the plot explicit with Charlotte Corday's legible note (Musées Royaux, Brussels).

Ingres insinuates his signature into his *Portrait of the Vicomtesse de Sennones,* 1816, on a trompe-l'oeil visiting card (Nantes museum).

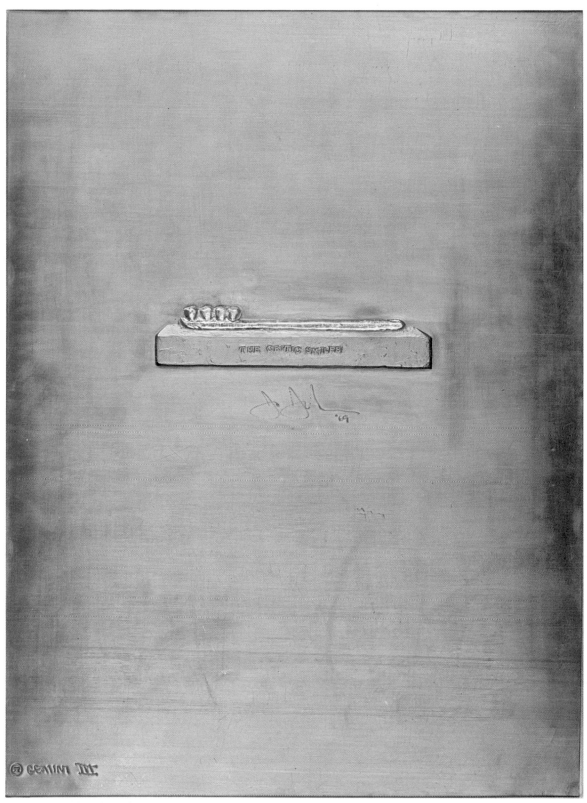

Jasper Johns: *The Critic Smiles,* 1969, lead relief,
23 inches high. Gemini G.E.L., Los Angeles.

EXHIBITING PAINTINGS

ALMOST EVERY PAINTER ARRIVES AT THE STAGE WHEN HE
WOULD LIKE TO EXHIBIT HIS WORK.
IT IS A GOOD IDEA TO HAVE YOUR PAINTINGS SHOWN
WITH THOSE OF OTHERS; IT GIVES YOU A FRESH PERSPECT-
IVE ON YOUR WORK, BECAUSE IT IS SURPRISING HOW
DIFFERENT YOUR PICTURES LOOK ON THE WALL SURROUND-
ED BY PAINTINGS OF OTHER ARTISTS.
SOMETIMES YOU ARE AGREEABLY SURPRISED WHEN YOUR
PAINTING HOLDS ITS OWN IN COMPARISON.
AT OTHER TIMES THE PAINTING THAT SEEMED SO COLOR-
FUL AND STRONG IN YOUR STUDIO LOOKS DRAB
AND WEAK ALONGSIDE OTHER PICTURES.

John Baldessari: *Exhibiting Paintings,* 1967,
67 3/4 inches high. Feigen Gallery, New York.

image in the framework of myth or fiction. Here language is present as a form of social action.

Promising, swearing, asserting and denying are verbal acts, not merely symbolic behavior. They are commitments, and formally bind the speaker to an ongoing context. "Will you marry me," is not conversation. The person who asks it is doing something. In logical terms, Magritte's painting is not simply words and image, A + B; it is (A + B). It is a confrontation in which verbal and visual processes clash. We find it as impossible to refrain from "seeing" the pipe as it is to avoid reading the words. Nor can we evade the confrontation by saying, "It's not a pipe, it's a picture." The painting is so sensually barren as to deny even Michael Fried a formal esthetic foothold. The tension between the words and the image is the focus of artistic interest, as the title suggests.

Whether or not it uses words, conceptual art engages us with language in this way. Lawrence Wiener's photograph of a bleak landscape with a personally fragmented rock in it becomes a work of conceptual art when it is read with its title, *The Arctic Circle Shattered*. Bruce Nauman's cast of an apparently arbitrary section of his body becomes conceptual art when we read its name: *Hand to Mouth*. These titles are constituents of the work. To see them as visual banality and verbal clichés neatly evades the point, which lies precisely at the intersection of word and image: the dissonance of two flat tones in violently dissimilar timbres heard simultaneously. Conceptual art is impersonal and forbids identification, more Brechtian than Brecht. Artistically, it submerges both subject matter and style, as a Borges short story submerges character and plot. Instead, the artist addresses his audience with the

One of Duchamp's works where word-play is the key: *Apolinère Enameled*, 1916-17, is a transformed ad for Sapolin enamel (Philadelphia Museum). And the title is the clue to how to look at Whistler's mother—as *Arrangement in Grey and Black, 1* (Louvre).

Miro writes *Escargot, Femme, Fleur, Etoile* in his tapestry cartoon, 1934, 77 inches high. Collection Juncosa de Miro, Palma de Mallorca.

Magritte contradicts himself in *The Treason of Images*, 1928-29, which he inscribes "this is not a pipe" (23¼ inches high). Collection William N. Copley, New York.

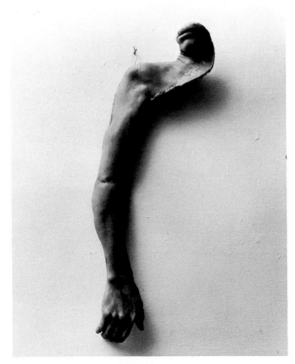

Bruce Nauman illustrates *From Hand to Mouth* with a wax cast from his own body, 1967. Collection Joseph Helman, St. Louis.

Bernar Venet is also his own subject in *Head Details, Working Drawing*, 1968. John Gibson Gallery, New York.

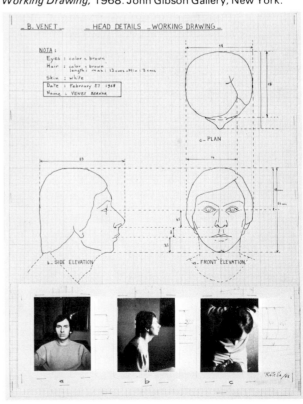

pseudo-gravity of scientific or intellectual detachment. We are given graphs, photographs, tables of numbers or words—proposals, orders, questionnaires to fill out, as in Donald Barthelme's *Snow White.* These solemn harbingers of knowledge, piled up on each other, collaged, overlapped, juxtaposed and intersected, yield no knowledge, but only stumbling-blocks to that purely rational intelligence that we call art. Instead of eroticizing technology, Barbarella-fashion, conceptual art uses ironic language to mock it and its claim to represent ultimate reality. And just as modern writers flout the fictional matrix in favor of essay, parable, enquiry, catalogue or investigation (Kafka, Mailer, Pynchon, Barth, Barthelme), so do these artists drop concern with pictorial space and form (nor are they involved with sculpture). This is a scruffy art—words fall on the page with all the distinction of dandruff on a blue serge suit. The ornamental handling of language, bijoux attitudes toward calligraphy and book production have nothing whatsoever to do with it. Its innovations are syntactic. Words and images are not separate material realms. They are treated as comparable outcroppings of the human condition, as equal and unequal as nails and hair. Verbal and non-verbal images are indifferently vehicles for thought.

We can't know what words tell us in pictures until we have some idea of how language works. Modern concern with rhetoric and public images is very recent. All language used to be thought of as a kind of naming, and truth was a matter of calling things by their correct names. The really interesting things about language—its relationship to behavior, action and theory-construction—were not considered to be linguistic matters. Today communication seems a more important matter than abstract truth. A new importance is attached to metaphor, for instance. Metaphor is no longer seen as a poetic device, but as an intricate, far-ranging method of intellectual construction.

Is it a lie to say that time is a river? How can we begin to think about something as abstract and real as time? If we liken it to a river, emphasizing its irreversibility, we will make other discoveries than if we think of it in terms of the seasons, where the cyclic, clock-like aspects of temporal change are brought to mind. As long as we think of time as something occurring outside ourselves, the concept of relativity is impossible to grasp imaginatively. Relativity requires more complex metaphors.

Some visual images clearly serve as non-verbal metaphors. They organize our minds and feelings. Their relationship to thought and language is as varied and complex as the relationship of verbal abstraction to examples, illustrations and models. I would like to invite the reader to look the five pictures on pp. 62-63 from the point of view of trying to figure out how we know what these pictures "say." Because, mysteriously, we do know what they mean, but we have no explanation of what we know or how we know it.

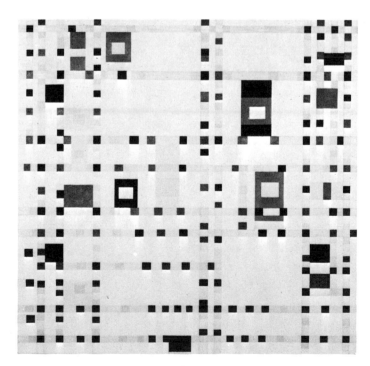

Late Mondrian becomes allusive: *Broadway Boogie Woogie,* 1942-43, 50 inches square. Museum of Modern Art, New York.

Not an abstract drawing, but a scenario for an earthwork: Dennis Oppenheim's *Ground Systems,* 1968, 19 inches high. John Gibson Gallery.

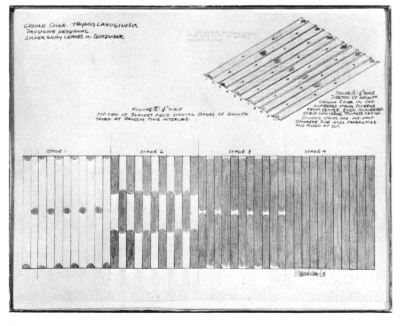

71

One of the 72 Dhyani or "meditative" Buddhas, eyes downcast, inside
its perforated stupa on a top platform. Photo by Joan Lebold Cohen.

By Eleanor Munro

Tales of Borobodur

The great and mysterious monument of Buddhist art, built by master craftsmen and architects in Java while Europe was still in the Dark Ages, incarnates the story of man's fate

The meaning of its name is lost in history, and at first glance the Borobodur looks its age: a thousand-year-old colossus of rotting grey stone flung together on a hill in the Dieng Plateau of central Java. Rice paddies and banana groves extend around it as far as the eye can see. At the limit of the fields stand guardian volcanoes, some smoking and others banking the fire which once laid waste to hundreds of shrines contemporaneous with the Borobodur. Now half buried, half overgrown with jungle as the Borobodur once was, these were mostly dedicated to the Hindu triad Shiva, Brahma and Vishnu and, in spite of their often luxuriant sculpture, were based on the conventional Indian temple plan of square, open courtyards with interior cells. Among these, Borobodur was unique, and unique it is even among monuments of the world: part Buddhist reliquary or stupa, part pyramid, aligned to the four directions according to magic recipe, it possesses a richer store of narrative sculpture than any building on earth and is as continuing a symbol of the twin universes we enclose, and are enclosed by, as any built by man. Even today, it seems to hold mysteries—to suggest something about outer space and inner necessity—which we shall never finish exploring. Along its six square flanks are Buddhist reliefs too numerous to digest. Seated above these, and on the top round terraces, 504 stone Buddhas tell another tale in the pantomime of their mudras, or hand-postures. Finally, the interlocked geometry of the whole has its own secret to reveal.

Borobodur was built for a dynasty of princes, the Caliendras, who moved from northeast India down to Sumatra and thence to Java, where they ruled from 778 until 864, carrying the word of Buddha which was, by the ninth century, fast fading from the Teacher's homeland. In Nepal, however, some late Buddhist cults took on new vitality as they mixed with

Author: Eleanor Munro, former managing editor of *Art News Annual*, is completing a history of Far Eastern art.

Tibetan Tantric ideas. At the Nalanda monastery, not far from Bodgaya, where Buddha sat beneath the Bo tree, more than a thousand monks from as far away as China and Java gathered to teach and discuss the holy Sutras, and to supervise the manufacture of little bronze figures of the Buddha in his by then many esoteric incarnations. It was this late, complex brand of Mahayana Buddhism which was disseminated through Sumatra and Java by the Caliendras.

For monkish pilgrims and princely believers in the cults, much of what seems obscure in the Borobodur today may have been an open book. So perhaps we too should come to it as pilgrims, imagining how seagoing Buddhists from the Ganges ports tacked down into the arms of the monsoons, touching at Sumatra, at last pulling their ships onto the Java coast. Then they would have pushed on by foot and big-wheeled wagon into the heart of the Pearl of the East.

At dusk, the paddies of central Java radiate a paradisiacal, green-gold color. As the Bima Express from Djakarta descends out of the highlands of Bandung into the plateau, we slowly are enclosed in this light, and at the same time, we feel peculiarly elated. Suddenly it matters little whether these rails lead to Compostela or to Borobodur. We might as well be passing through olive groves on our way to Delphi. For we have entered the universal Pilgrimage Tale. Only since all gods are equally strange to us—Buddha no more, no less, than those of Olympia or Eden—it will be the "psycho-physical pilgrimage," as Rowland calls it, which will be, for us, the Borobodur's theme.

For over 900 years, no pilgrim came to the monument. Not more than six decades after it was built, the Borobodur and all the shrines around it were abruptly abandoned, no one knows why, and the jungle crept out to cover it. Through the eighteenth century, while Moslems and then the Dutch merchants of the East India Company ruled Java, none of them suspected what was hidden under that enormous green hump. Then in 1811, for only four and a half years, there came to Java as governor Stamford Raffles, one of those organizational geniuses of the India Service with lively curiosity about the regions he had been appointed to rule. Raffles was especially struck by ruins in the middle of the island which, as he later wrote, "dwarf to nothing all our wonder and admiration at the pyramids of Egypt." Those near the village then called Borobodo he found particularly promising: a bristly mound of broken stones, roots of trees and vines from which projected hundreds of "naked figures sitting cross-legged and considerably larger than life." Yet the real meaning of the Borobodur's iconography escaped him. All he could venture was that it seemed "in style and ornament much to resemble those of the great Budh temple at Gai-ya on the continent of India." He sent out an engineer, Cornelius, to rip away the jungle and make a report, so that when the Dutch returned to their posts in 1816, the monument stood clear. By 1823, the Hollanders had got to work on their own, beginning by sending at least two heads of Buddhas around the Cape of Good Hope to the Ethnographical Museum in Leyden where they rest today. Soon it was established beyond doubt that the figures were by their "long ears and Negroid hair" to be identified as Buddhas, but still the whole building with its veils on veils of relief sculptures did not seem to present a unified theme but simply an assemblage of "adventurous legends of Rama," or perhaps of "King Radjuno, a warrior who, after fighting many battles and gaining endless victories, retired from the world to a mountain." These were the speculations of another Englishman, William d'Almeida, who preferred to call the romantic ruins by the name Boro Bodoo.

There the question rested. Then in 1835, the linguist Karl Wilhelm von Humboldt, nearly blind and chairbound after a life of exploration which had led him to the South Seas, turned back to a subject he had long mulled over: the old Javanese language, Kawi. Forgotten since the Moslem conquest, Kawi was commonly used when the Borobodur was built. Humboldt, like Darwin and Herbert Spencer whom he preceded, believed there existed a process of universal organic evolution or, as he put it, that "in the last analysis, human activity follows no other goal than the pursuit of understanding of Law." Since Kawi was derived from Sanskrit—a language with a true system of grammatical forms—and since the Borobodur was invented by Kawi-speaking men, it seemed inconceivable to Humboldt that the monument, too, should not illustrate a single Law. All its random-seeming details, he felt certain, were embroideries upon one theme, forgotten in his time, but somewhere clearly stated in the philosophy which gave rise to it.

With the most ancient form of Buddhism—the Hinayana teachings which had spread into Ceylon—Humboldt could find no connection. But there was a particular esoteric system, developed in eighth and ninth century Nepal, which seemed promising (though at that time little was known of the actual historical ties between this region and Java). At the heart of this cosmological system existed an "Adi" or highest, intangible, purely mental Buddha, from whose meditations were extruded, as it were, a constellation of lesser Dhyani, or "meditative" Buddhas. These in turn set the universal wheels of the Law into play. And so, from their mental labors, the whole universe of evolving forms was called into existence. To Humboldt, the iconography of the Borobodur—especially the top platforms with their mystifying burden of 72 Buddhas hidden inside stone stupas—seemed point for point to reflect these doctrines. Since his time, scholars have disputed minor issues: which precise shade of the Buddha—Vairocana or Vajrasattra or another—really is represented in the stupas; and who, really, is the little pilgrim so ardently

One of the 160 reliefs around the base devoted to the realm of *Kamadhatu*, world of undirected, uninspired men; here, ugly, deformed people who do nothing but talk.

F.C. Wilsen's frontispiece drawing for a book
on Borobodur published in 1874 in Leyden, one of
a series that is the earliest complete record.

Borobodur, section The monument is built right over
the earth hilltop, of slabs of rock without cement.
At bottom, right is shown the foundation wall hiding
the *Kamadhatu* reliefs, which some scholars believe
served to prevent the monument from sliding downhill
and others to cover the reliefs for doctrinal reasons.
The central, main stupa reaches 130 feet above the ground.

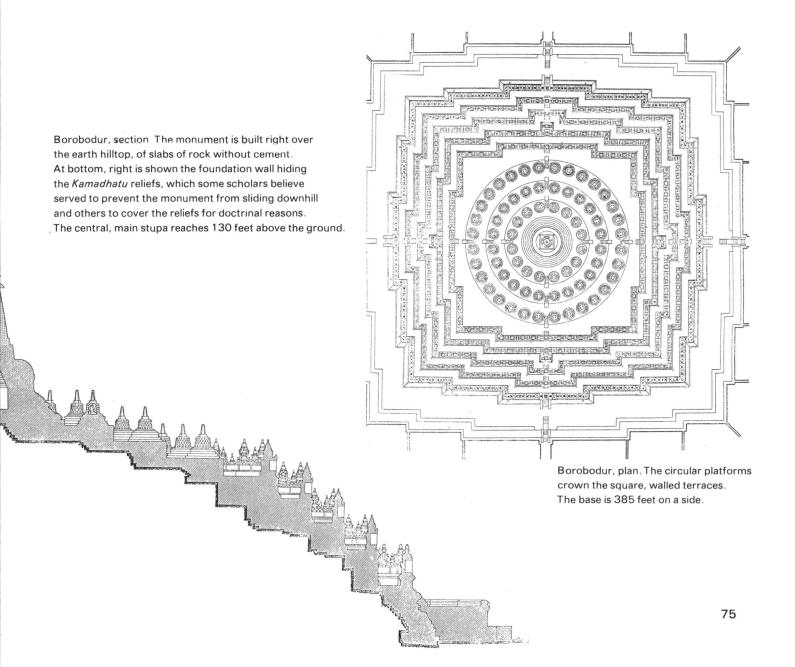

Borobodur, plan. The circular platforms
crown the square, walled terraces.
The base is 385 feet on a side.

A corner of the east façade, showing the lowest frieze of welcoming princes
and gods and goddesses—and above, the Buddhas in Touching-the-Earth mudra.

wending his way between miracles up the terraces; and what, exactly, was once inside the main stupa which, when Cornelius first climbed up and pulled aside the vines, had already been broken open and was, as far as he could see, empty. But it has not been doubted since that the Borobodur aims to represent the universe itself.

Realizing this, we can return to the pilgrimage road. We are driving out before dawn from the central Javanese city of Jogjakarta, toward ghosts of volcanoes which congeal out of the dark. It is 5:30 A.M. A saffron beam strikes the column of smoke rising from Merope, "Fire Mountain," dead ahead. The sky lightens a degree and Soembing stands up, cleft at the top like a broken tooth. Crowds of men and women in lavender and brown sarongs, with baskets on their heads, are pressing forward in the direction we are going, toward the village of Borobodur, where it is marketday. Brown ducks swagger in the gutters. A toy vendor whirls his red paper parasols, pulls a wooden flute out of his sack. Behind the rattan huts on each side of the road, mist lies on the rice and corn, the tapioca and tobacco fields. We cross a shaking bridge and look down into the muddy whirlpools of the Elo River; next the Praga, swift and flat. All travelers on the road to a particularly holy spot must first make their way through *samsara*, the "wandering world," where men go about their commonplace work.

By 6:15, we pull up a steep dirt road to a line of wooden shacks. Here the impoverished but dedicated Indonesian Archeological Service has its headquarters, fighting (funds are promised, but not yet forthcoming, from UNESCO) to save the Borobodur from total ruin by dismantling, then rebuilding it.

We get out of the car, find ourselves beneath tall trees lightly shaking in the cool air. The skies are pale and the branches filled with singing birds. But where is the famous monument we have come so far to see?

Here is no Gothic cathedral with wide-open portals to welcome us, no Greek temple with easy platforms splashed by sun. A sprawling, aged mass, it seems to hunch its shoulders and turn its back on us. Splotched with lichen and stone cancer, it clutches the ground with clumsy lower ramparts, then rises through a forest of monotonous spikes to a top tower so wrapped in fog it seems to belong to another world.

A Bo tree, dripping dew, stands inside the east entrance to the grounds. We breakfast in its shadow, sitting on rocks next to a Buddha which has rolled out of its niche and now harbors some spiders and a big striped snail. We drink our coffee and study the ramparts, trying to decide how to enter that bristling confusion of forms.

Suddenly the sun breaks over the horizon behind our backs, shining full strength against the façade, and a vision of Buddhas—92 facing outward on each side—leaps into focus. With morning light on their chests, they reach as one down to touch the ground, as in the Bhumisparca mudra: "'I gave up much in a former life,' said Mara, God of Evil, of

Tales of Borobodur

Detail of the lowest frieze, female figure
with flywhisk and incense burner.

Gargoyle waterspout to carry off the tropical rains.

One of the steep, forbidding staircases running up the
middle of each of the four sides of Borobodur, by which
the pilgrim makes his way from terrace to terrace
to the open platform on top and the huge main stupa.

The dream of Queen Maya
announcing the conception.

The future Buddha as young Prince Siddhartha bestowing
his ring on the maiden Gopta, his bride-elect.

Tales of Borobodur

Queen Maya, attended by nobles and servants, on the way to Lumbini park where the miraculous
birth of Buddha occurs. Above and right, others of the 120 reliefs depicting Buddha's life, the *Lalita Vistara*.

The Prince receives from his father King Suddhodana three palaces for the different seasons and more by-wives.

King Suddhodana indulges the Prince with women, who fall asleep around him in unseemly attitudes.

The temptation of Buddha by the daughters of Mara.

The Buddha meets his five former comrades in a hermitage and converts them to faithful disciples.

things in the wandering world, but who is there to attest that thou hast sacrificed to find the Truth?'

"The Bodhisattva answered, 'I appeal to this mother of creatures.' And he touched the earth.

"The whole earth shook, and a million myriads of goddesses appeared. And Mara and his hosts fled in all directions."

Now we see an entrance to the monument, a kind of cleavage in the cliff and steps which seem to have been hacked into it. But first, the sullen foundation wall...

From this, a rock tumbled down one day in 1885. Behind it, and as he later found continuing all around the monument, the then Chief Engineer of the site, J. W. Ijzerman, discovered a row of reliefs which had been carved and then sealed off while the building was still under construction. These 160 reliefs are devoted to samsara—or, in Buddhist doctrine, the realm of *Kamadhatu,* world of undirected, uninspired men in the flatlands of life. Carved with brutish simplicity, these squat, animal-like men and women fight and hunt, go to market and till the fields. Wicked and good are there together: bugler and fisherman, ascetic and housewife, drummer and king. Questions of ethics have not yet occurred to them, yet punishments await the sinners: Eight Hot and Eight Cold Hells are pictured in all their horror, and also, the reincarnations that await evil-doers in this life: the angry man finds himself reborn as a leper, the lustful one as a woman. Along the rims of some

a word or two carved in Kawi still remains. *"Virupa,"* says one: "deformed" or "ugly." "Rich landowner," specified another, and "Gift of an umbrella." These were notations by the master-planner to local artisans who, apparently, were assigned subjects and left to compose and finish the panels as they wished.

Now climbing the first stairs, we see before us only one frieze of reliefs turned face-outward: a row of gracious figures arranged in simple triads: a man between two women flanked by two more. They hold rosaries and lotuses, censers and flywhisks, beckoning us to come up beyond *Kamadhatu* into *Rupadhatu,* the "Realm of Forms" evolving from the naturalistic toward the abstract, where, bit by bit, we will find our way out of the world's net.

We turn left into the first sculpture terrace to begin *"pradaksina"*—the pilgrim's rite of circumambulating the holy monument in a sun-wise direction, and the façade rises up as if to swallow us. On our left, it shuts out the view. The path turns sharply. We forget how we came in and have no idea where we are headed, except that the seated Buddhas guard the way and, at the top, the great Stupa waits. At our right, along the Borobodur's body, a heavy cornice flows forward, crowded with lesser stupas and scrolls, gargoyles and chains of flowers. But what overwhelms us so completely that we feel hopeless to try to absorb them are the relief panels which

One of the Jataka stories telling of Buddha's incarnations
in animal forms in earlier epochs, to help mankind.

spill out on each side, two deep, 1,400 in all by the time we will
have climbed to the limit of *Rupadhatu.*

At our right shoulder begins the story of the life of Buddha.
There are 120 scenes, all of them translations into stone of a
particular Sutra, the *Lalita Vistara,* which sets the scene for
his miraculous birth by introducing the elder gods making
plans in their Tusita Heaven, and proceeding through the
stages of his life until the First Sermon in the Deer Park of
Benares: "There is a middle way," he began...

In style and treatment, the reliefs differ as the workmen
differed: some are roughly modeled, devoid of ornament,
with figures in clumsy poses; others show the figure of Prince
Siddhartha, who became the Buddha, in perfect Gupta style,
undulantly graceful among clouds of angels strewing the air
with flowers. In composition not unlike Early Christian ivories,
with which they share a Greco-Roman root, these sometimes
crowded, flattened panels are alive with natural forms—
deer and birds, trees in full leaf, pools of water and symbolic
mountain peaks.

At our left, and beneath the Buddha legend, unroll Jataka
tales, stories of miraculous happenings in the course of former
incarnations of the Pilgrim who, in our epoch, was born as
Gautama Buddha. He has come as other gods, as a wandering
monk, as an elephant to let hungry men feed on his flesh, as
a bird singing his sermons from a tree. There are almost 500
Jataka stories on the Borobodur.

We climb and turn through three more square terraces.
One describes another pilgrimage, that of the boy Sudhana,
scion of a South Indian house. According to an ancient tale
popular all the way from India to Japan, he left home to sit
before 64 gurus in 110 towns until at last he learned how to
become a saint. Then we climb to the level of the First Buddha
of future worlds: Maitreya, and from there, into the ambiance
of an even more rarefied Buddha-spirit, Samantabhadra, the
Last Buddha of eternity. Gradually the panels have become
less complex. Where earlier ones showed bending archers
and ships in sail, apsaras and dancers, now the Bodhisattvas
stand placidly side by side, extending their hands in blessing
or lifting them to teach.

Four times we have turned to the four directions and been
aware that the 92 Buddhas of each façade make different
hand-gestures related to the kind of terrain they overlook
(prescribed as well by the Dhyani Buddha system). Each of
these mudra-making Buddhas, moreover, represents a separate aspect of the god and oversees a separate department
of creation. To the East, the way we came, Buddha Aksobhya
touches earth to prove his willingness to give up much to find
the Way. South, Ratnasambhava looks out over a domestic
view of farms and a small valley. Over this tranquil scene, he
makes the mudra of Blessing. To the West, where once the
dormitories of monks and pilgrims probably lay, Amitabha,
Lord Buddha of the Western Paradise, who will save all men
of good faith, folds his hands in the meditation mudra. Finally,
to the north, a long view of open fields lapping against the
volcanoes and, beyond them in our mind's eye, the ocean
with its danger and challenge, Amoghasiddha lifts his hand,

A Jataka happening: attack upon a princely residence
with garlanded pillars and storied buildings.

Tales of Borobodur

Another of the more than 500 Jataka episodes
from the upper square terraces of Borobodur.

Jataka tale involving a dancing girl and a
royal personage, with orchestra at left.

Looking out from the top of Borobodur, south to southwest. Note the square openings in the stupas of the highest ring, as against the diamond-shape openings in those of the lower two.

The view upward through the three rings of beehive stupas hiding Dhyani Buddhas to the big main stupa. What it once contained—if anything—no one knows for sure.

Tales of Borobodur

View of the top of Borobodur
before restoration.

A Dhyani Buddha, its stupa lost, with hands in Turning-the-Wheels-
of-Law mudra. Spiral, curls and long earlobes are marks of Buddha.

its palm turned outward, in the mudra which says Fear Not.

Southwest of the Borobodur is a jagged range said by the villagers to show the profiles of the building's master-architect, one Gunodharma. Nobody knows who he was or where he came from, with his mandala for blueprint and his vision of ascending levels of material and immaterial worlds. But no less symbolic was his setting of the Borobodur into the landscape in such a way that, as Melville said when he climbed the Acropolis, "in the site, the horn of hills, is some greater truth about the building..."

Only the summit lies ahead when we leave *Rupadhatu*. A transitional terrace tears us away from the sculpture-laden squares to the cold circles of the top. Now we are free of walls, at the level of the tallest treetops. From here, we can see at our left a beating counterpoint of urns and stupas on the cornice we have left behind and, along their backs, one farewell repeated design, of urns bearing garlands of lotus, carved in relief as shallow as a wing. "Peace," the symbol says, and "peace" again. And then we are in the empyrean terraces. The stupas of the first two ranks have diamond-shaped windows; the last are square, as if even these small emptinesses can be brought to a condition of greater rest. Inside, fitfully lit, the Dhyani Buddhas make their complex finger positions denoting the Turning of the Wheels of the Law.

According to pre-Buddhist Indian cosmology as well as to Tantric teachings based on mandalas, man and the cosmos were intimately inter-related. Earth was a square bounded by mountains. Beyond lay the formless collective waters from which we emerge for our hour of consciousness. In the middle,

upright as a man's spine, was Mount Meru, ridgepole of the universe and symbol of Law which holds all things in their places. Now against the sky, the only form higher than ourselves is the trunk of the Borobodur, Meru's peak.

Nobody knows what it originally contained. Some say only a ritual vessel or two, a bronze pilgrim's bowl for example, or a holy water pitcher. Others think a stone or gold figure of Vairocana or Vajrasattva, or one of a Caliendra ruler as Deva-raja, god-king. Or it may have been a particular unfinished Buddha which stands today at the foot of the monument. At some time in the 1840s it was found inside the stupa, broken and half-buried in sand, and it has suited the sense of order of some scholars to see in it a symbol for the godhead who lent his shape to Man.

It is left for us to confront the possibility that, beyond the rising ranges of form which are the Borobodur, at the core of this nebula, there may well have been nothing at all we could lay our hands on—that the Pilgrimage needs no ephiphany, that the upper terraces are simply, as Rowland says, "the most eloquent representation art could devise of the great void which is the creator and last home of the soul that has wandered down worlds so long and wearily."

Or is our epiphany to be found somewhere within the fact that, once we have made the journey from samsara to open, unpeopled distance, we are not allowed to stay? We are not Simon Stylite and cannot spend our lives upon the bronze umbrella which once shaded this magic mountain. The deep, steep steps take us back down, fast, to the level of the work-men and the road, where an ancient green bus clatters by on its way to market at Borobodur village.

Scenes from the *Passion of Christ,* page from a late 6th-century
North Italian Gospel believed to be one of the books
Pope Gregory dispatched to St. Augustine to convert the people of
Britain to Christianity. Corpus Christi College, Cambridge.

84

By Carl R. Baldwin

Making the Word Material

How medieval artists were able to turn cathedrals into 'bibles for the illiterate' and still express the ideal of a Divine presence 'Whom we neither show nor see'

Around the year 600, Pope Gregory reprimanded a bishop of Marseilles who had permitted wall paintings in his church to be destroyed, fearing that they were becoming the object of veneration: "We allow pictures in churches so that men who cannot read can look at the walls and read there what they are unable to read in books."

Gregory's conception of art as a "Bible for the illiterate" may read like a motto from one of today's textbooks on medieval art, but it represented only a slim majority view at the time of its enunciation. In the first centuries of our era many writers attacked the very notion of Christian representational art, and during the entire Middle Ages artists had to be ingenious in finding mediums and materials that would not run aground on the shoals of theological resistance to images. To appreciate this ambivalent attitude towards representational art, we must try to imagine ourselves as early Christian artists and theologians, surveying the monuments of pagan Antiquity and trying to figure out where to go from there.

In the Roman Republic, Cicero had noted the "sculpted likenesses of gods and statues of old men" (*"simulacra deorum, statuae veterum hominum"*) that will be familiar to any museum visitor. The orientation towards *simulacrum* and *statua* in Roman art naturally called for large-scale sculpture in the round, either in marble or bronze. Under Augustus, the Imperial notion of unlimited power began to unfold, as well as the idea of the descent of the Emperor from the gods. When the Christian Faith was adopted and promulgated by the Emperor Constantine and his successors in the fourth and fifth centuries, these inherited conceptions underwent a sweeping conversion. Many statues of gods and goddesses were destroyed outright, since they were believed to contain

Author: Carl R. Baldwin teaches medieval art history at Lehman College of the City University of New York and is writing a volume on Carolingian illuminated manuscripts.

demons. Some Christian accounts, collected and analyzed by Cyril Mango, lead us to believe that the precipitate departure of the demon could cause the spontaneous destruction of the sculpture. In 402 A.D., for example, Bishop Porphyry of Gaza approached a much venerated statue of Aphrodite with a crowd of the Faithful bearing Crosses: "the demon who inhabited the statue, being unable to contemplate the terrible sign, departed from the marble in great tumult, and, as he did so, he threw the statue down and broke it into many pieces."

Christian wrath must also have been aroused by those bronze and marble statues of Emperors which had been employed to enforce religious conformity. A letter to the Emperor Trajan from Pliny the Younger, governor of Bithynia around 110 A.D., explains the details of this procedure: "Those who denied they were or had been Christians, who repeated after me an invocation to the gods and offered incense and wine to your image (which I had ordered brought in with the images of the gods for the purpose), and who, moreover, cursed Christ—it is said that no real Christian can be forced to do these things—I thought it right to dismiss. Others said they were Christians but soon denied it...They all venerated your statue and the images of the gods and cursed Christ." These bitter associations of bronze and marble statuary with a threat of martyrdom will help to explain the widespread destruction of statues in this early period, and the lingering suspicion of figural representation harbored by Christian theologians in this and later periods.

In many cases, certain details of Imperial imagery could be saved by adroit conversion. The figure of Jupiter, represented as god of the sky with a billowing canopy, is emblazoned on the breast-plate of *The Emperor Augustus,* and appears again, under the feet of the youthful, smooth-cheeked *Christ Enthroned* on the Sarcophagus of Junius Bassus. The Christian of fourth-century Rome would have had no difficulty in deciphering the meaning: Christ replaces the Emperors as the chosen ruler of the universe, the "Emperor of Emperors." In the panel below, *Christ Entering Jerusalem* is a rebuttal to the Imperial triumphs which had glorified military victory, displayed captured booty and occasioned long, festive holidays in the capital city. In this sculpted stone coffin, the Christian Gospels (the word means "good news" or "glad tidings") promising Eternal Life replace the Imperial panegyric.

But the imagination of Christian artists was not challenged for long by such neat conversions of ancient Roman motifs. Christian art, after all, is something more than Roman-style figures stripped of armor and equipped with Crosses. What was far more difficult and challenging was to develop mediums and styles that could suitably express the Christian idea of sacrifice, redemption and peace. In the opinion of some theologians, the idea defied visual expression. In a penetrating study of the Iconoclastic tendency within early Christian thought, Ernst Kitzinger has quoted the argument of Minucius Felix, a writer of the early third century: "What image can I make of God when, rightly considered, man himself is an image of God? What temple can I build for him, when the whole universe, fashioned by his handiwork, cannot contain him? Shall I, a man, housed more spaciously, confine within a tiny shrine power and majesty so great?" And further on: "But surely the God whom we worship we neither show nor see."

Such writers feared that Christians would be tempted to worship Christian images in a manner uncomfortably similar to the ancient worship of statues of the gods: statues of Christ or a saint might be regarded as embodiments of the Divine, to which (or to whom) prayers and offerings could be brought. Around the year 200, Tertullian referred to image-worship as "the foremost crime of the human species," and had this to say about image-makers: "Whenever and wherever the devil has placed sculptors and painters in the world, idols have sprung up and caused calamity to men." A writer of the fifth century, Epiphanius, made the following laconic and bitter observation: "When images are put up, the customs of the pagans do the rest."

If images were to survive at all, the task of the Christian artist was clear: to develop mediums and methods to depict

Right: Emblazoned on an initial page of the Lindisfarne Gospels, England, ca. 700, are the first three letters of the Greek name of Christ, XPI. British Museum, London.

Marble statue of the *Emperor Augustus*, ca. 20 B.C., as a simulacrum of a god. Vatican Museum, Rome.

Christ Enthroned and *Christ Entering Jerusalem*, detail from the sarcophagus of Junius Bassus, 359 A.D., marble, about 42 inches high. Museo Sacro, Vatican Museum, Rome. At the feet of *Christ Enthroned* appears the same effigy of Jupiter as on the breastplate of Augustus (right).

Incipit euangeli um secundum mattheu::

cryster

uutedlice
ruce per
cryster cnou
re ro

god lice

cynn ꝑcce me re t cnou resu   ruce ꝺur   ꝑer   mið ꝟ

RATIOXICGERATIOM

ꝑer   bi poeðdeð t beboden t bepartnud t betaht

ESSETCSBOUSATA

moder   ꝟr

MATER EIUS MARIA IOSEBR

Iconic image of the Forerunner of Christ: *St. John the Baptist*, ivory plaque, 10 inches high, detail from the Chair of Bishop Maximian, 545-553 A.D., probably from Constantinople. Archepiscopal Museum, Ravenna.

the heroes of the Faith without provoking idolatrous reactions. The Christian in Rome or Constantinople, breathing an air which had been, so to speak, polluted by a millennium of idols, should breathe freely of the rarefied air of the *imago* (or, in Greek, *icon*)—the Holy Picture which would inspire meditation and reverence, but never provoke those reactions of idolatrous worship which a darkened previous age had encouraged.

How to do it? Life-size sculpture in bronze and marble was eliminated altogether, and small-scale works in wood, metal and ivory took their place. In these works, artists made it clear, through the use of low-relief carving rather than sculpture in the round, that an image of a Holy figure was intended, not a statue which attempted to simulate a real man or god—not, to use the vocabulary of Cicero and Tertullian, a *statua* or *simulacrum*. It is not accidental loss, then, but artistic intention that must explain the fact that we have not a single statue of Christ, the Virgin, the Apostles, saints or angels from this period that was carved in the round: the age-old conception of the *statua* or *simulacrum*, that tempter of idolatry, had to be destroyed. In this respect Christian thought harmonized with the Biblical proscription of idols. "Thou shalt not make unto thee any graven image," the Lord commanded Moses: "Thou shalt not bow down thyself to them, nor serve them."

The distinction between *statua* and *imago* will be clear if we compare the statue of *The Emperor Augustus* with the sixth-century ivory relief of *St. John the Baptist* from the Chair of Bishop Maximian in Ravenna. The formalized, flattened figure of the Baptist holds a roundel showing a lamb,

the Symbol of Christ, and points upward as if to advise the believer to study the scenes from Christ's life carved on the *cathedra*, and to ponder the Sacrament of Baptism. This is an *imago* or *icon*: a life-size marble or bronze of the Forerunner of Christ in the Baptistery would have been a *simulacrum*, and would have been banned—even if a latter-day Phidias or Myron had commandeered the sculpture workshops of sixth-century Ravenna.

With all these associations, it is apparent that sculpture could not be the most suitable medium for the expression of the Christian concept of an encompassing spiritual presence. The ideal medium for the expression of Christian thought in the Mediterranean was mosaic. It is not a Christian invention, to be sure: acres of floor and wall mosaics decorated the palaces and baths of Antiquity in Italy and North Africa and Syria. But in Antiquity it was used as a sort of durable translation of naturalistic painting: decorate the floor of your dining room or bath house, and be able to trample on it or scrub it down for a life-time without maintenance worries. In Christian art, the medium not only rises from the floors to decorate nave walls and apses (and, in later Byzantine art, domes): its naturalistic function is abandoned and it becomes an enveloping spiritual presence. From a host of tiny colored glass or marble cubes a vision materializes that cannot possibly be mistaken for a *simulacrum*. The reflective property of the materials, and especially of the vast background panels of blue or gold, nullify corporeality and impose upon the observer the concept of *imago, icon*.

In this medium, Imperial imagery could be retained through conversion. Indeed, the subtler aspects of the ancient Roman

A Virgilian eclogue crystallized into a Christian image: *The Good Shepherd*, mosaic lunette in the Mausoleum of Galla Placidia, 450 A.D., Ravenna.

Making the Word Material

Old Testament scenes prefiguring events in
the life of Christ are depicted in this
12th-century enameled and jeweled cross,
21 3/8 inches high, by Godefroid de Huy,
Meuse valley. British Museum, London.

The pathos of Christ's death is heightened by
the light blue of the head contrasting with
the stark white of the body, in this champlevé
enamel *Crucifix,* Limoges, 13th century,
22 3/8 inches high. Metropolitan Museum.

notion of the *Pax Romana,* which were never susceptible to expression in large-scale sculpture, could be presented for the first time. In the fifth-century mosaic of *The Good Shepherd* in the Mausoleum of Galla Placidia in Ravenna, Virgil's Fourth Eclogue—"herds of sheep will not fear great lions... The serpent, too, shall perish"—has been Christianized and crystallized. The beardless, Apollonian Christ is garbed in the gold and purple that was the exclusive privilege of Emperors, and the ancient gesture of command has been transmuted to a caress. The conquered barbarian yielding to the Roman general on the breast-plate of Augustus has given way to the sheep protected by Christ, and these animals, turning their eyes to the shepherd, are images of the *anima,* or souls, of the Faithful. This translation from Roman commander to Christian guardian is unthinkable without the development of an anti-sculptural medium.

The vaults framing *The Good Shepherd* mosaic are decorated with circles and crosses scattered on an intense blue ground which gleams with subdued radiance at the slightest infusion of daylight from the single entrance door below. Not an image, only, but an environment has been created—and one which accords with Minucius Felix's evocation of an invisible, measureless Being.

New tasks require new mediums, and the challenge of converting the peoples of the British Isles to Christianity in the sixth and seventh centuries—"to make Angels out of Angles," in Pope Gregory's phrase—generated a flurry of activity in writing and illustrating the Scriptures. One of the books that Pope Gregory probably dispatched to Augustine, the sixth-century bishop of Canterbury, is now in the Library of Corpus Christi College, in Cambridge, England. This Gospel Book of St. Augustine includes a page with 12 *Scenes from the Passion of Christ,* beginning with Christ entering Jerusalem (upper left) and concluding with Simon of Cyrene bearing the Cross (lower right). This page, with three square panels in each of four horizontal registers, is framed by a simulation of veined marble (modeled to suggest volume) and constitutes a small-scale imitation of wall painting. "Pictures in Churches" have been reduced to portable size, and remain strictly in line with Pope Gregory's definition of the usefulness of images.

Gregory's idea of a "Bible for the illiterate," however, is remarkably transformed in the art of the British Isles during the seventh and eighth centuries (referred to variously as "Insular" or, to give some notion of the mixed Irish and English contributions, "Hiberno-Saxon" or "Anglo-Irish" art). Narrative scenes from the Bible are virtually unknown in this art, and what is emphasized instead is a nearly magical quality of the Sacred Word, and, within an individual word, the embellishment of initial letters. The decorated metalwork of the "barbarian" peoples who spread through Europe in late Antiquity was crucial to this new conception of letters and words: the idea of a personal adornment of precious metal, suitable to a chief—a shield, sword hilt, belt buckle or purse lid—was rapidly converted to the decoration of metal book covers and parchment pages. And the labyrinthine, interlaced ornament found in the burial sites of chieftains—the treasure of Sutton Hoo, in Suffolk, is the most splendid example that has come to light—found its place in the carpet pages and initial decoration of Christian books.

In a page from the Lindisfarne Gospels, a north English manuscript of ca. 700, the initial letters *XPI* (the first three letters of the name *Christos* in Greek) are enormously attenuated, and their extremities spin off into the page in a manner that recalls the whorls and spirals on embossed metal shields.

The whorls and spirals of Celtic metalwork are carried over into the sinuous movement of the *Lion of St. Mark* on this title page of the Echternach Gospels, North England, ca. 700. Bibliothèque Nationale, Paris.

A stork bending over to seize a snake in its bill forms the initial P, first letter of *Pistevo* (I believe) beginning the text of the Creed, in this page from the Sacramentary of Gellone, Meaux, end of 8th century. Bibliotheque Nationale, Paris.

This conception of the initial letter as an animated, flexible form, capable of extravagant growth or sudden shrinkage, carries over to the Insular conception of human and animal forms. In the Echternach Gospels, a manuscript made in north England and sent to the Continent ca. 700, the lion of St. Mark is like a gigantic initial, full of surprising compressions and inflations—the chest expands, the waist narrows, and the tail coils like a reversed S.

Manuscript painters in France during the eighth century began to respond to Insular ideas, while continuing to express a native propensity for letters made with birds and fish. In some cases—as in the Sacramentary of Gellone, made near Paris ca. 800—it is hard to reconcile some of the decorated letters with the dogmatic function of the manuscript. How are we to explain the Sacramental function of the interlaced and entangled bird and serpent forms of the letter P of one of its pages? The P belongs to the word "Pistevo" ("I believe") which begins the text of the *Credo,* enunciated here in Greek words that are transcribed in Latin letters (a Latin *Credo* appears on the facing page). Instead of an instructive illustration of the benefits of Faith, the artist gives us a conglomerate initial dominated by an extremely limber crane bending double to catch a tiny knotted snake. Unless we interpret this detail as a veiled illustration of the Virgilian and Christian prediction that "the serpent, too, shall perish," we must admit that dogmatic illustration has been subordinated to an artist's improvisation and fantasy.

There were, to be sure, certain limitations on artistic invention, and the function of the Sacramentary of Gellone was well served by a depiction of the *Crucifixion* at that passage in the text which noted the identity of Christ's body and blood with the Eucharistic bread and wine. What is especially notable about this Western conception is the fusion of figures and objects with letters and words: the Cross must be read as the initial T of TE IGITUR CLEMENTISSIME PATER ("You, there-

fore, most merciful Father"), words that are uttered as the priest makes the sign of the Cross over the bread and wine ("depicted" by three small Crosses in the text adjoining the Cross). Pope Gregory's dictum has been observed here, but this fusion of letters and picture, of "Word" and "flesh," could never have been imagined by a Mediterranean Pope or artist.

A far more naturalistic and painterly rendering of the same theme occurs in a Carolingian Sacramentary of the ninth century that may have been made for the Coronation of Charles the Bald, a grandson of Charlemagne. The Sacramental character of the image is stressed by the gatherings of blood in tiny, grape-like clusters. Here, also, the Cross is treated as the T of TE IGITUR, and its role as an initial is emphasized by the terminals that expand into interlaced scrolls.

During the period from 726-787 A.D., scenes from the Life and Passion of Christ were officially banned from Byzantine art, to be replaced by the austere image of the Cross, set in gold against a blue mosaic ground. The Iconoclasts argued that artists working with earthly materials were capable only of representing the human and mortal nature of Christ, and not the Divine and immortal nature: the arrogant attempt to render the two natures of Christ in material form was worthy of anathema. Also heretical was the attempt to render beings like angels and cherubim that were entirely divine, and lacked any mortal or material component.

In 787 A.D., the Byzantine Empress Irene convoked the Second Council of Nicaea and reinstated the use of images (Iconoclasm was renewed from 815 until 843, then definitively abandoned). A bungled translation of the Council minutes, from Greek into Latin, led Charlemagne and his advisors to believe that the Byzantines had renounced image-breaking only to fly to image-adoration. The Carolingians' rebuttal to this supposed idolatrous policy was contained in the *Libri Carolini,* 791 A.D., in which they opposed both Iconoclasm and Idolatry. In arguing for the use of images, the Byzantine

The cross of the Crucifixion serves as an initial in this page from a Carolingian Sacramentary believed to have been made for the coronation of Charles the Bald, St. Denis, mid-9th century. Bibliothèque Nationale, Paris.

Making the Word Material

Text and image are intimately mingled in this page from the Sacramentary of Gellone, Meaux, France, end of 8th century. Bibliothèque Nationale, Paris.

Council had pointed out that Moses had decorated the lid of the Ark of the Covenant with two cherubim of wrought gold. The Carolingians, thinking that the Byzantines had quoted Scripture to encourage image-worship, explained that the Cherubim of the Ark were not objects of adoration, but symbols of the "consonance" of the Old and New Testaments.

Some of the Carolingian arguments concerning images seem to be paralleled in certain pages of our two Sacramentaries. The image of the *Crucifixion* in each manuscript answers the Iconoclast argument against employing the material substance of paint to render a nature that is both human and Divine, and the two cherubim that flank *Christ in Majesty* in the later Sacramentary may be a double-edged sword: opposing the Iconoclast view that Divine Beings defy material representation, they may also embody the Carolingian view that such representations have an edifying symbolic connotation and need not provoke adoration. By showing cherubim, the artist seems to be illustrating the conviction of the Carolingians that they, and not the Byzantines, were properly in line with God, Moses and Pope Gregory in allowing "pictures in churches" without succumbing to idolatry.

If manuscripts were the ideal medium for the dissemination of Gospel truths and correct liturgical practices during the seventh, eighth, and ninth centuries, architecture and monumental sculpture assumed this role in the twelfth century. The central portal of the west facade of Chartres Cathedral, ca. 1150, includes a number of elements that we have already seen in Gospel Books and Sacramentaries. The symbols of the Evangelists that spring across the pages of Insular books are here gathered around the central figure of Christ on the tympanum. The idea of showing the Man, Eagle, Lion and Bull as winged creatures holding the books of their Gospels is a carry-over of the Carolingian idea of refuting Iconoclasm by rendering Beings of immaterial nature in material form. Indeed, the development of portal sculpture in

France reveals a Western willingness to solidify Divine Beings into three-dimensional form that never suited the Byzantines, with their preference for flat church exteriors and mosaic-clad interiors.

In contrast to mosaic makers or manuscript painters, the sculptors at Chartres were not dealing with a flat surface and a simple rectangular or arched format, but with a surface zig-zagging into the Cathedral wall and animated by 63 projecting figures of changeable scale. All of the figures are marginal in the sense that they are placed above or beside the central space of the entrance door, and the task of the sculptor was to create order and clarity out of what could be a confused babble of forms. His solution involves the beauty of number— a poem in stone on the harmonious relation of one to four. The single Christ is placed at the center of the tympanum, flanked by four Evangelist Symbols; below, 12 Apostles (flanked by two Prophets) line the lintel. In the archivolts, 12 angels in the inner channel are framed by 24 crowned and bearded men in the outer two channels. Below, eight jamb figures originally flanked the entrance doors (an unadorned column replaces a missing figure on the left jamb). Symmetry is absolute: a plumb line dropped from the top of the archivolts would divide each category in half—except for the indivisible Christ.

More than a consonance of numbers is involved, however. The jamb figures are Old Testament Kings, Queens and Priests who foreshadowed elements of Christian dogma, and the 24 crowned men holding an impressive array of medieval stringed instruments are crucial to the meaning of the portal: they are the Elders with crowns and citharas who adore the Lamb, in St. John's Vision of the Apocalypse. The subject of this central portal, then, is not the *Christ in Majesty* that we know from the Carolingian Sacramentary, but the *Christ of Judgment.* This reading of the central portal—the main entrance to the church—permits us to grasp the pertinence of the

Christ in Majesty flanked by cherubims, page from the Sacramentary of Charles the Bald, 9th century. Bibliothèque Nationale, Paris.

sculpture to the dogmatic function of the Cathedral as a whole.

If the exterior sculpture conveys a clear dogmatic message in emblematic form, the interior plays more upon irrational aspirations than intellectual preoccupations. Once the impression of extreme darkness wears off, the observer finds himself "dwelling in some strange region of the universe which neither exists entirely in the slime of earth nor entirely in the purity of Heaven"—a region of the mind that Suger, the twelfth-century Abbot of St.-Denis, discovered through the contemplation of jeweled chalices, but which is even more easily provoked by the environmental art of Gothic stained glass. Within the Cathedral, it is "not lessons but illuminations" that fill the mind and eye, as Louis Grodecki has pointed out.

Metalwork assumed the role of a small scale, legible accompaniment to the sonorous, multicolored curtains of glass. In contrast to the stone sculpture embedded in exterior walls, metalwork shrines and crucifixes were either flat or adorned with figures in precious substances that defied any association with *statua.* The champlevé enamel *Crucifix* in the Metropolitan Museum should be imagined on an altar, where it would have provided a miniature reflection of the golds, reds, greens and blues of the stained-glass walls.

In the champlevé enamel technique, parts of the metal plaque are scooped out to provide "pools" for colored paste, which is melted into a hard, glassy medium. Between the "pools," metal walls remain to draw golden lines and separate color areas. In this *Crucifix,* the death of Christ is made explicit by the light blue color of the head, in contrast to the stark white of the torso and limbs. Melted paste is gathered in "pools" of white and blue for flesh and tunic, while the curved, repeated lines of ribs and muscles are given by the thin metallic walls.

The image of the dead Christ—emphasizing the *pathos* and human nature of Christ—was permitted in Byzantine art after Iconoclasm, and alternated on equal terms with the open-eyed, alive Christ. This alternation is also employed in Western images (the open-eyed Christ, for example, occurs in an enamel in the Cleveland Museum of Art which strongly resembles the one at the Metropolitan). The notion of a Divine nature and a triumph, however, is stressed by the resplendent, unearthly qualities of the champlevé enamel medium.

Within the cathedrals, then, towering volumes are filled up with insubstantial color, and only small objects clustered around altars—enameled shrines and crucifixes—are legible. An environmental art is created which, along with the mosaic walls, apses and domes of Byzantine art, comes as close as material substances can to expressing the notion of Divine presence—that Being "Whom we neither show nor see."

Presiding over the Old Testament figures and Elders of the Church, the sculptured Christ in Majesty
of the west portal of Chartres cathedral, ca. 1150, becomes the Christ of Judgment of the Apocalypse.

Intruding into this landscape is the human profile Dürer discovered
in his view of the *Fenedier Fortified Rock at Arco,* 1495, watercolor
and gouache, 8 11/16 inches high (above and detail left). Louvre, Paris.

By Patrik Reuterswärd

The Face in the Rock

Chance images and visual puns in Renaissance and Mannerist
art sometimes were mere scholarly games, but
they were also used to expose deeper levels of content

On his way back from Venice during spring 1495, Albrecht Dürer, riding along the slopes of the Italian Alps, stopped here and there in order to capture the great views. One of his first halts seems to have been Arco, north of Lake Garda, where the painter spent a morning depicting the great rock with its stronghold and the houses and olive groves below.[1] The result was one of the first and most beautiful watercolor landscapes in history. Oddly enough, this lovely picture discloses an enormous face in the wall of the rock, which by its conspicuousness leads one to suspect that it was the primary motive of Dürer's watercolor.

This naïve delight in discovering as well as inventing faces and figures where there should not be any at all is time-honored in Western civilization. A remarkable case, though far from the earliest, is that of the provincial Roman stone-mason at Bordeaux who, getting tired of submitting to the classical system of decoration, made the foliage and rosettes of a cornice develop into fantastic face-like shapes.[2] The same impulse later urged a Carolingian book-illuminator to turn the marble veins of some columns of the canon tables into rude, not to say intrusive faces.[3] Probably the artist enjoyed making them as much as the monastic beholder enjoyed discovering them. A few centuries later, a South-German illuminator had the ground surrounding the Holy Family likewise animated with faces with probably no further purpose than that of mere fun.[4] Such examples might seem to be revelations of the naïveté of the medieval mind, yet chance images occur even more frequently in Renaissance painting. Since Lorenzo de ' Medici explicitly enjoyed them,[5] it is no wonder that Signorelli had a cloud in his *Great Pan* shaped as a rider on his horse.[6] Mantegna did the same in his *St. Sebastian* in

Author: Patrik Reuterswärd, curator at the National Museum, Stockholm, recently completed a book on Hieronymus Bosch.

Vienna, and in one of his mythological paintings in the Louvre the clouds clearly appear as faces.[7]

Needless to say, these pictorial puns were hardly more than pleasantries, intended to entertain and distract the noble beholder. Also Dürer cannot have taken it very seriously when, on that splendid morning in 1495, I believe he intentionally painted the face in the rock. Yet a chance image tends to destroy its physical or pictorial environment. The moment you are aware of its presence, you cannot get rid of the face, or whatever form it may be. Indeed because of the chance image in the rock, Dürer's watercolor loses a great deal of its charm. This destructive rule applies to most pictures where such puns occur—after the discovery of faces in Mantegna's clouds, the beholder cannot honestly turn them into clouds again and the painting will remain pictorially unsatisfactory. One might say that such an additional image within the image works effectively only when it is not too conspicuous.

Dürer may gradually have become aware of this, because among all the highly definite objects of his intentionally ambiguous *Melencolia I*, there is one figuration which is not definite at all. On the large upper surface of the polyhedron, the light shading is unevenly applied, leaving out an amorphous shape which slightly resembles a face or even more a skull. Since it is the only amorphous spot in the engraving, I believe it was added to serve as a *memento mori*.[8] Dürer often alluded to Death and Vanity, and his contemporaries sought such allusions everywhere.

This would not have been the first instance of a death's-head being inserted as an intended chance image. In the Hours of Catherine of Cleves, ca. 1440, it is already present, in all its horror, on the underside of the wing of a butterfly.[9] Here the chance image is no longer mere play, but serves as a deeply felt reminder of mortality, all the more so as it appears in connection with a butterfly, symbol of both the soul and the brevity of life. As the late Prof. Panofsky has made clear to us all,[10] there was in the Netherlands a definite wish for

Standard classical foliage and rosette decorative motifs are metamorphosed into human faces in a Gallo-Roman cornice, 3rd-4th century A.D. Musée d'Aquitaine, Bordeaux.

hidden messages in pictures. To decide whether the chance image, too, when used as a message, should be regarded as hidden or not, is no crucial matter. Some of the disguised symbols which have been unraveled by Panofsky are in fact not hidden at all, since they reveal themselves by their very absurdity. I am thinking of two of his most famous cases, Jan van Eyck's device of letting the light shine from the north in the church of the Berlin Madonna as well as the same painter's ingenious idea of letting the Virgin of the Annunciation answer the angel with letters which are rendered upsidedown: INᗡ ∀ᒥᒥIↃИ∀ ƎↃↃƎ.[10a] Rather than speaking of a disguised symbolism, one may say that an additional message in these cases is being transmitted by means of a postponed release. Only after a while do you discover that there is something wrong with the picture, and you have to find the explanation for it yourself. Chance images when used as messages work very much the same way.

It is strange that they were not used to a greater extent for this purpose. Beside the death's-head already mentioned, the sure cases known so far are apparently few. One specimen is by Dürer's Swiss friend Hans Leu in his *St. Jerome in the Desert* (in Basel). The hermit has leaned his crucifix against an old willow, which in its upper section bears the likeness of Christ's head crowned with thorns.[11] Having discovered this figuration, the beholder senses the presence of the Savior more intensely than the tiny crucifix would imply. Through this serious image within an image, the agitated forms of the scenery get a profound motivation, as if the Redeemer was omnipresent in the picture.

The message in the face of Leu's painting need not disturb as chance images otherwise tend to do. Its effectiveness comes from its very ambiguity, which is an advantage rather than a shortcoming—we may again think of Dürer's *Melencolia I,* in which the face on the polyhedron would have been a complete failure, had the outlines been perfectly clear and unequivocal. Chance images when used as messages demand prolonged contemplation; they enter the beholder's mind as an additional insight.

It goes without saying that Hieronymus Bosch, too, was aware of this means of communication. However he was not satisfied with a mere curiosity to find faces in the forms.[12] Bosch realized in fact that other images and signs could be used as well. His non-anthropomorphous chance images occur in two works which deserve special attention here.

We all know *The Peddler,* that enigmatic picture in Rotterdam, also known as *The Prodigal Son.* The representation

No more than pure diversion are the faces that mingle with the marbling of the columns of Canon Tables (left and detail below) in this page from the Carolingian Gospel Book of St. Médard, Soissons, ca. 800. Bibliothèque Nationale, Paris.

Entirely unrelated to the scene of *The Nativity* are the heads arbitrarily inserted in this illuminated page of the St. Blasien Psalter (left and detail below), South Germany, ca. 1230. H. P. Kraus, New York.

looks perfectly consistent, and yet we hesitate at all sorts of absurdities which, we understand, are present in the picture in order to make us try and recollect. There is, for instance, that ridiculous jug placed upside-down on the peg of the roof—who could have placed it there? It suffices to say that the jug in this connection denotes something evil about the house, which through other details is clearly characterized as a brothel.

An oddity on the same absurd level is the fact that there is a gate without a fence.[13] Bosch seems to have wished the beholder to pause and consider the riddle of the gate. Its answer has been given by Lotte Brand Philip,[14] who noticed that the beams of the gate are arranged into a definite, perfectly readable pattern: in whichever direction you choose, the beams form the well-known angular pattern of a gallows. The reading will be confirmed when we shift over to the house, on which the same curse is repeated four times in the half-timber work as well as in the outlines of the gable, which directly corresponds to the diagonal beam of the gate. Consequently, the *sens morale* must be: Those who lead this kind of a life are bound to end disastrously sooner or later on the gallows.

The same technique of narrative occurs in the little Prado picture of *St. Anthony in the Wilderness.* Wilhelm Fraenger, the highly disputed, yet greatest of Bosch interpreters, noticed that the old oak in the center bears in its upper part a resemblance to the skull of a stag, with the branches forming a pair of antlers.[15] The oak no doubt holds a secret. Knowing of the use of the stag in Renaissance imagery, Fraenger gave this cranium sign a sexual significance—and probably correctly. The painting shows St. Anthony at his favorite place under the tree, but without that tempting woman who usually turns up at his side. Bosch has apparently replaced her by

the tree-skull in order not to spoil the meditative mood of the picture. The conflict of the story told here is, in fact, mainly a conflict on the level of contemplation.

St. Anthony is represented as an old, hardened hermit who would hardly succumb to those mischievous agents of evil which approach him from all directions. We need not worry much about their rather futile threats. Still, in order to make the saint's ultimate triumph clear to everybody, Bosch had the lantern of St. Anthony's chapel in the background replaced by a real helmet. Large and blue as it is, this absurd helmet turns the chapel into something of a stronghold, as if to assure us that St. Anthony will not be defeated.

This technique of adding signs and objects as additional hints was developed by Bosch alone. Other painters of his and the following generations followed far simpler schemes. In those few cases where the chance image is not playfully inserted, but acts as a reminder, the message is always the same: Death. There are, for instance, landscapes where an entire mountain has been transformed into a gigantic death's-head. Contrary to Bosch, who had no use for skulls and hourglasses, his contemporaries and the following generations cherished this kind of symbolism.

The most famous of all death's-heads is the one in Holbein's portrait of the *Two French Ambassadors* in London. It works as an image within the image, though without being a chance image in the proper sense. The picture offers in fact two separate paintings, one (the portrait of the ambassadors) intended to be viewed from the front, and the other (the obliquely intersecting, distorted death's head) intended to be seen from the side. The painting was most likely meant to be placed high up in a gallery.[16] On entering, the beholder at first glimpsed only the death's-head, which, as he approached the center of the painting gradually went out of focus, giving

Common in Renaissance painting are visual puns with hidden meanings, such as the cloud in the form of a horseman in Mantegna's *St. Sebastian*, ca. 1458, 26 inches high; Kunsthistorisches Museum, Vienna (left and detail far left). The image is based on a Romanesque bas-relief in Verona and is believed to allude to the Ostrogothic king Theodoric, 5th-century conqueror of Italy.

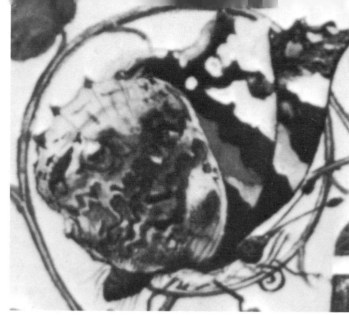

Intentionally ambiguous among the clearly delineated objects in Dürer's famous engraving, *Melencolia*, 1514, is the shading resembling a skull-like face on the polyhedron, possibly to serve as a *memento mori* (left and detail above).

On the underwing of a butterfly, itself the symbol of the ephemeral, appears the image of a death's head, in the margin of a page from the Hours of Catherine of Cleves, ca. 1440 (left and detail above). The Pierpont Morgan Library.

way to the front-view picture of the two young but nonetheless mortal diplomats.

This combination of images is an early example of an anamorphosis, that savant game with double perspectives which the following generations of the sixteenth and seventeenth centuries so delighted in. Even though the optical play was a sufficient end in itself, there is at least one more case where such a combination of perspectives has been used with the purpose of adding a message. I am thinking of a strange picture at the Dayton (Ohio) Art Institute, which has been attributed to the Antwerp master Gillis Mostaert.[17] In its main view, the painting displays a disastrous panorama, probably *The Last Days of the World*, but when viewed from the lower right, the foreground turns into a crowned giant warrior falling on his sword. Whatever precise meaning this suicide is intended to stand for, it seems quite clear that it carries a message which is part of the main theme of the picture.

As for chance images proper, as they occasionally occur in sixteenth-century imagery, they should not be treated as mere isolated tricks. They are in fact part of that tendency towards the fantastic, which determines so many landscapes of the period.[18] Already in the fifteenth century extraordinary rocks occur in the pictures, some of them with quite impossible tunnels and projections. Whatever the roots of this trend may have been, it continued throughout the sixteenth century as a kind of reaction against true observation. A picture was not accepted as beautiful unless it was enhanced by such extravagant elements, among which the chance image was

but one of several resources. For that reason, it does not always matter much whether the rock actually shows a face or not, as long as it adds the fantastic note to the picture.

Chance images nevertheless continued to be made with the definite intention of being understood as such.[19] But the whole practice came almost to an end by way of overdose through Giuseppe Arcimboldo towards the end of the sixteenth century. Where before him certain rocks had been given human features, Arcimboldo turned the whole landscape into a half length bust. And the same is true of his many still-life settings with human forms—one cannot tell any longer which image is within the other. Nor can one speak merely of symbolism here—the whole picture carries a symbolical significance, image has become allegory. Uncompromisingly, and with a strong sense of both the destructive and vital forces of life, Arcimboldo went on producing these weird allegorical portraits, which, taken together, seem to cover a whole system of thought. There are, for instance, his frequently copied series of The Four Seasons and The Four Elements, which fitted perfectly into the system of the princely *Kunstkammers* of the period, whereas some of his other "portraits" epitomizing The Library, The Winecellar, The Kitchen, etc. illustrate the components of a princely household.

The pun may appear plain, particularly when repeated from picture to picture. Yet it would be unjust to Arcimboldo to judge his works only from the point of view of variation. Their intention was as serious as any philosophical treatise of that

Hieronymus Bosch's *The Peddler,* also called *The Prodigal Son,* ca. 1490-1500,
27 5/8 inches diameter (Boymans-van Beuningen Museum, Rotterdam), is full of
seemingly nonsensical details that together denote the absurdity of life.

Bosch's *St. Anthony in the Wilderness,* ca. 1500, 39 inches high (Prado, Madrid) is invested
with strangely allusive imagery: the dead oak over the saint's head resembles the
skull and antlers of a stag, which had well-known sexual connotations in the Renaissance.

period, and when looking at his self-portrait in Vienna, one gets a feeling of how earnest he was. At times, too, Arcimboldo deepened his message by adding to the allegorical whole a further significance, as can be demonstrated by a remarkable picture at Skokloster, Sweden. The painting, commonly known as *The Gardener*, would have fitted well well into a set of panels which already comprised *The Cook, The Librarian* etc., had we not Gregorio Comanini's word that it actually was intended as a eulogy to the Emperor himself, Rudolph II.[20] Comanini, who was a friend of Arcimboldo's, eloquently describes the picture as an allegorical representation of the Emperor in the guise of Vertumnus, the god of seasonal riches and changes, who according to Ovid was himself capable of undergoing many metamorphoses. When combining the sovereign with the idea of Vertumnus, and not with that of Apollo or Hercules, as was the general rule, Arcimboldo surely also had in mind the mental instability of his venerated patron. After having re-established this connection or identity, the beholder may even have been tempted to regard the picture as a portrait, despite its lack of Habsburgian traits.

We may hope, however, that the Emperor, to whom the painting was sent together with Comanini's text, did not understand it as a simple likeness. Without having penetrated the whole problem, I would, however, suggest that His Im-

perial Highness accepted being hailed as a Vertumnus. How are we otherwise to explain the fact that the court painter Georg Hoefnagel, when designing Rudolph II's emblems a few years later, loaded them with cucumbers, turnips, flowers and fruits?[21] Still, much remains obscure. We know nothing of the original placement of the picture. It may have been hung in the *Kunstkammer* together with The Four Seasons, denoting, by its larger size, Vertumnus as a ruling principle. But it could also have hung alone, or together with one of Arcimboldo's *Floras*—in the latter case, however, with the consequence that the beholder would have started inquiring about the identity of Flora as well.

We began with Dürer and Bosch, who were among the first to trouble the naturalistic setting with an additional image of consequence, in Bosch's case quite definitely with the purpose of transmitting a message. Having experienced the realm of Arcimboldo's double projections, we have reached the threshold of the seventeenth century, a period when precious talks in front of the pictures became almost a social rule. Paintings and murals were treated as hardly more than pretexts for airy eloquent expositions.[22] A situation arose quite contrary to that of the Renaissance artist, with the consequence that painters who had something important to convey, henceforth would be doing well to express it straight.

In *St. Jerome in the Desert*, attributed to Hans Leu, 1515, the top of the old willow against which the hermit has leaned his crucifix bears the likeness of Christ's head crowned with thorns (left and detail above). Oeffentliche Kunstsammlung, Basel.

One of the earliest and most famous examples of that optical play of perspective called anamorphosis occurs in Hans Holbein the Younger's *Two French Ambassadors*, 1533, where the obtrusive object in the foreground is immediately recognized as a skull when glimpsed from the side, but becomes illegible in the front view. National Gallery, London. The detail on p. 106 shows the anamorph corrected by a camera aimed almost parallel to the surface.

The tendency toward the fantastic in 16th-century landscape is reflected in this Flemish
panel, *Portrait of Don Quixote,* ca. 1650, 15 3/8 inches high, where the terrain
takes the form of a horse (right) and a man's profile (left). Galerie Flinck, Brussels.

The Face in the Rock

1. That the watercolor was made during the morning of a day in spring has been corroborated by people who know the site. See F. Winkler, *Die Zeichnungen Albrecht Dürers*, I, Berlin, 1936, p. 70, no. 84.

2. For further information about these extraordinary fragments, see L. Valensi's entries to nos. 2 and 3 in the exhibition catalogue *Bordeaux Gallo-Romain*, Chambéry, 1969.

3. Paris, Bibliotheque Nationale, Ms. lat. 8850, fol. 12b (Evangelary from St. Medard at Soissons). H. Ladendorf, *"Zur Frage der künstlerischen Phantasie,"* in *Mouseion*, Studien aus Kunst und Geschichte für Otto H. Förster, Cologne, 1960, p. 24, fig. 13. I am indebted to H. W. Janson, New York, for this reference. Prof. Janson has himself dealt with the problem of chance images in "The Image Made by Chance in Renaissance Thought," *De Artibus Opuscula*, XL, Essays in Honor of Erwin Panofsky, New York, 1961, pp. 254-66, and in an article in the *Dictionary of the History of Ideas*, which should appear this year.

4. H. Bober, *The St. Blasien Psalter*, New York 1963, pl. IV (fol. 7v). Prof. Janson kindly drew my attention to this manuscript.

5. W. Welliver, "Signorelli's *Court of Pan,"* *Art Quarterly*, 24, 1961, p. 344 note 27.

6. For an illustration, see last year's Art News Annual, *Light*, p. 126.

7. Janson, op.cit., 1961, pp. 262ff.

8. P. Reutersward, *"Sinn und Nebensinn bei Dürer. Randbemerkungen zur 'Melencolia I'",* in *Gestalt und Wirklichkeit,* Festgabe für Ferdinand Weinhandl, Berlin, 1967, pp. 411ff.

9. J. Plummer, *The Hours of Catherine of Cleves*, New York, 1966, pl. 129 (p. 268). Pierpont Morgan Library, New York. This interesting instance of a chance image with a definite purpose was kindly pointed out to me by Prof. Janson, New York.

10. E. Panofsky, *Early Netherlandish Painting*, Cambridge, Mass., 1953.

10a. Panofsky, op.cit., pp. 138 and 147f. I doubt, however, that Panofsky's explanation to the letters written upside down ("so that God in His Heaven can read it") really hits the point. At any rate, this device may as well serve to indicate, as does the light shining from the North, the supernatural qualities of the Annunciate, implying that Her voice and words simply cannot obey terrestrial rules. For the same reason, though in a diametrically opposite context, the monstrous eagle at the gates of Orcagna's Hell on the walls of Sa. Croce, Florence, utters his *"Lasciate ogni speranza"* with letters running backwards (R. Offner, *Corpus of Florentine Painting*, IV:1, New York 1962, pl. III[12]).

11. It has been pointed out by E. Castelli, in *Umanesimo e simbolismo*, Atti del IV convegno internazionale di studi umanistici, Padua, 1958, pp. 19f.

12. Whether intended or not, there is something of an evil face to the right in the Eden panel of the triptych of the *Garden of Delights*. Anthropomorphous features are also in the rock to the right in the main panel of the *Haywain*. I might add an observation, which a student at Chapel Hill, Gaillard F. Ravenel II, made in 1968 about the main panel of the *Garden of Delights*. He suggests that the whole landscape has been given the outlines of a reclining woman. It is indeed an imaginative observation which deserves serious attention. The whole scene is ruled by a female principle, as indicated by the Luna symbol in the center. For a more detailed investigation, see my book on Bosch, in the Uppsala series *Figura*, 1970, pp. 76ff.

13. This inconsequence was first noticed by K. Seligmann, "Hieronymus Bosch: The Peddler," *Gazette des Beaux-Arts*, 42, 1953, p. 98.

14. L. Brand Philip, "The Peddler by Hieronymus Bosch, a study in detection," *Nederlands Kunsthistorisch Jaarboek*, 9, 1958, p. 72.

15. W. Fraenger, *"Die Versuchung des heiligen Antonius, Madrid,"* *Hessische Blätter für Volkskunde*, 49-50, 1958, pp. 20ff.; also in *Archivio di Filosofia*, 3, 1957, pp. 155ff., and *Castrum Peregrini*, 32, The Hague 1957-58, pp. 15ff.

16. J. Baltrusaitis, *Anamorphoses, ou perspectives curieuses*, Paris 1955, p. 65.

17. Baltrusaitis, op.cit., p. 16f.; *Fifty Treasures of the Dayton Art Institute*, Dayton 1969, p. 72.

18. For a further analysis of this phenomenon, see G. Marlier, *"Pourquoi ces rochers à visages humains? Le paysage anthropomorphe se situe au point de rencontre de l'inquiétude religieuse et de l'hallucination paienne,"* *Connaissance des Arts*, June 1962, pp. 82-91.

19. As one of the more extreme cases, I wish to mention an anonymous Flemish landscape from the early seventeenth century, at Galerie Robert Finck, Brussels, Exposition 12, 1969, no. 14. On the right, the whole terrain attains the shape of a horse, whereas on the left, the landscape turns into a bearded face.

20. G. Comanini, *Il Figino o vero del fine della pittura*, Mantova 1591, pp. 31-43; S. Alfons, *"Giuseppe Arcimboldo," Symbolister*, II, *Tidskrift för Konstvetenskap*, 31, 1957, pp. 134ff. Being published in Swedish, this extensive monograph on Arcimboldo has not been sufficiently acknowledged.

21. As shown on fols. 1v and 13 in the *"Schriftmusterbuch"* of George Bocskay (Kunsthistorisches Museum, Vienna), the decorations of which were made by Hoefnagel for Rudolph II 1591-94. See figs. 17 and 22 in Th.Wilberg Vignau-Schuurman, *"Die emblematischen Elemente im Werke Joris Hoefnagels,"* Leiden 1969, a comprehensive iconographical study, which, however, does not undertake a consideration of the Vertumnus symbolism suggested here.

22. For the extreme of this tendency, see J. Montagu, "The Painted Enigma and French Seventeenth-Century Art," *Journal of the Warburg and Courtauld Institutes*, 31, 1968, pp. 307-35.

When viewed from a sharp angle, the foreground of *The Last Days of the World* (15 3/8 inches high), attributed to the 16th-century Antwerp Mannerist Gillis Mostaert, shows a king falling on his sword (left and detail below). Dayton (O.) Art Institute.

Image becomes allegory in Giuseppe Arcimboldo's *The Gardener,* or *Vertumnus,* ca. 1580, which is also a eulogy to the emperor Rudolph II. Skokloster Museum, Stockholm.

The mace-head of King Scorpion (detail), from the proto-dynastic Thinite period, ca. 3000-2778 B.C., depicts an actual historical episode, the ceremonial opening of a canal by the king.

By H. A. Groenewegen-Frankfort

'Narratives' in Ancient Egypt

The problem of the narrative element in ancient Egyptian art extends to the role of the pharaoh, who was first a god among gods, and later a god among men

The inverted commas in our title mean rather more than a hint that the term "narrative" should not be taken too literally in connection with Egyptian art. They are intended to point to a strange paradox: apparently those delightfully garrulous artists who in painting and relief have told us so much about man's work, his play and his entertainments avoid, with the exception of one brief revolutionary period in the New Kingdom and its aftermath, pictorial narrative. But since this term is somewhat ambiguous we shall, at the risk of appearing pedantic, insist on more precision in its use.

A narrative or story told is the verbal re-presentation in a coherent form of an *event*, real or fictitious, significant or trivial. This simple definition has two important implications: *a*) a story is concerned with a particular occurrence; a static situation or a typical act does not provide a story; *b*) in the process of being told the occurrence is "unfolded," in other words its successive phases have organic coherence. Strictly speaking, therefore, the term "pictorial narrative" should only apply to those illustrations of an event where its phases are presented by the only pictorial means available, namely a juxtaposition of actual episodes, a common procedure in Assyrian and medieval art, for example, which is continued to this day in strip cartoons. Even when a *known* story is evoked by depicting a pregnant moment in it, like Apollo's gesture in the pediment at Olympia, it should not be called a pictorial narrative. Egyptian artists, however, show a marked reluctance to illustrate the eventful in its transient aspect—with the one exception we already mentioned. Where events are

Author: Mrs. Frankfort, an archeologist who has worked on many expeditions in Egypt and Mesopotamia, is the author of *Arrest and Movement*, "an essay on space and time in the representational art of the ancient Near East" (Faber & Faber). A second edition shortly will appear in this country.

recorded at all these are more often than not deliberately robbed of their dramatic actuality. We hope to show not only how this was done but why Egyptian artists were so disinclined to "tell a story."

After these preliminaries it must seem ironical that the first relief we shall discuss can only be called an attempt at pictorial narrative. In fact it succeeds with charming naïveté in conjuring up an important event, the ceremonial opening of a canal by a king named Scorpion, a protodynastic ruler of Upper Egypt. The spatial relationship between the king—a dominating figure wielding a hoe—and his scampering subjects remains obscure; their gestures may or may not be simultaneous; in short as a "story told" it is vague and confusing, but the twisting stream and the landscape features scattered in an amorphous space lend actuality to the inadequate narrative; we seem to witness an event "taking place."

It was the last effort of this kind for a long time to come. When King Scorpion's successor, the almost mythical Narmer, commemorated his conquest of Northern Egypt by which he united The Two Lands (as Egypt was henceforth called), no attempt at pictorial narrative was made. On a large votive palette of slate the actualities of a great historical battle are ignored. The king's posture, mace lifted in one hand, a captive enemy held in the other, is not the prelude to an act, it is a symbolic statement of victory. As such it remained canonic for the representation of pharaoh's invincibility in ages to come.

What could have caused this sudden change? We can only suggest that the act of unification of The Two Lands brought about not only great political changes but a different concept of the function and significance of kingship. This may seem a rash statement since we lack all evidence for it during the first and second dynasties. Only in the third dynasty does the stupendous funeral monument of King Zoser at Saqqara justify the assumption that the classical Egyptian concept of divine kingship had found adequate expression. Although modern secularism is apt to emphasize the tyrannical aspects of this creed and to ignore its metaphysical implications, we shall deal mainly with the latter because they are relevant to our problem.

It has been proved beyond a doubt[1] that the royal function had cosmic connotations. It is for instance very striking that the term *ma'at,* which means divine order (as manifest in the stately rhythm of Egypt's undramatic climate) is also used to denote the order and justice on which human society depends, and which was maintained by Pharaoh's rule. The fact that cosmos and state were inseparable notions suggests that regal power had not simply an aura of transcendence—in Egypt it literally meant that the realms of the human and the divine coalesced in the person of the king. This "incarnation" of divine power made the inexorable fact of his aging and death unacceptable in human terms; it had to be minimized or denied. Hence the periodic celebration of the so called Heb Sed jubilee throughout the history of pharaonic rule, which entailed the king passing through a ritual death to have his power reaffirmed. At his death the transference of his power to a successor had to be dramatically enacted and his mortal remains preserved for eternity. If this should suggest similarity to well-known and almost universal primitive practices, Zoser's monument confirms that Egyptian kingship is not a monstrous outgrowth of magic rites but a challenging religious concept. In the elaborate architectural outlay at Saqqara, the king's pyramid-tomb was surrounded by exact replicas in stone of all those buildings—usually perishable structures—in which pharaonic rule had functioned during his lifetime. No transient event was depicted in the precincts of the monument, no act recorded. But one of Zoser's statues was placed in a closed *serdab* with slits at eye level. This affirmed that the counterfeit buildings, exposed to Pharaoh's eternally watchful gaze, still signified the scene of his superhuman function—notwithstanding the fact that the holy precincts were destined to be the undramatic stage for mortuary priests to perform their changeless, repetitive acts. What nevertheless prevents this paradoxical approximation of life and death from appearing a gigantic hoax and gives it a surpassing dignity is the emphasis on the *functioning* of the pharaoh's transcendent—truly divine—power. The entire architectural concept seems silently to proclaim John Donne's defiant creed: "Death thou shalt die."

We can now justify our assumption that the change of style in Narmer's palette reflected an altered concept of kingship, for his image appears to be the first step in the direction of the pharaoh's apotheosis. Not the king's act but his *being* victorious, his invincibility *per se* was here proclaimed (rather humbly as yet, on a votive object intended for a god). In time,

Hesi Re, the king's minister, at an offering table, wood, Old Kingdom, 2778-2723 B.C. Cairo Museum.

Rare attempt to depict an actual event: Battle and siege of town in war between the Egyptians and Arabs, drawing from a tomb at Deshasheh, 6th Dynasty, 2423-2263 B.C.

The votive victory tablet of King Narmer, slate, 25 inches high, Early Dynastic period, 3000-2778 B.C., is a symbolic statement of the Pharaoh's invincibility, without striving for pictorial narrative. Cairo Museum.

The Pharaoh as a humanized god: King Akhenaten and Queen Nefertiti
with their children, directly under the solar orb of the god Aten,
limestone, 12 inches high, New Kingdom, 1364-47 B.C. State Museums, Berlin.

however, the process of deification went far beyond Zoser's monumental statement. The emphasis on the royal function was entirely lost in the IVth dynasty. In Khafra's austere funeral temple the royal statues alone proclaimed his divine actuality by their potent presence. And when later in the Vth dynasty scenic reliefs were introduced the king was shown on a par with the gods, their equal not only in stature but in a curious relationship of reciprocal benevolence: the gods were supplied with offerings but they in return were shown leading Pharaoh's captive enemies.

All this confirms rather than denies a form of metaphysical speculation implicit in the paradox of a divine king. It is rooted in a desire to reconcile those perennially irreconcilable opposites, human and divine, ephemeral and eternal, life and death. In the royal monuments of the Old Kingdom a stupendous effort was made to affirm their conciliation. The king's eternal life-in-death was re-presented in stony effigies. The transcendent was equated with the permanent.

This grandiose quasi-solution, however, left the perennial problem on a human level unsolved. For Pharaoh's subjects, who could not emulate his divine status, the only solace was a devout trust in their god-king as a lasting beneficent power, a faith expressed in the traditional magic formula repeated in most private tombs: "an offering which the king gives."

There was, however, one feature of the Zoser monument that could be translated into simple human terms: the effigy of the dead king facing the architectural images that evoked the values of his life. In the more or less contemporary private tomb of a high official, Hesi Re, we find an admittedly rather different type of confrontation. On several wooden panels set in the niches of a long passage, the owner has been rep-

resented while on the opposite wall were depicted food, vessels and other chattels. The gift of various necessities of life, above all food, had been an immemorial custom (it took embarrassing proportions even in the precincts of Zoser's monument), but in the tomb of Hesi Re the mere presence in effigy of pleasure-giving objects was an innovation which proved the prelude of a remarkable development. Within a very short period the dead man's image was confronted not with chattels but with scenes of human activities such as growing food and the slaughter of cattle. A strict pattern was evolved: the large inactive figure of the tomb owner bracketed a number of registers on which these activities were depicted. The relation between the owner and the scenes was explicitly stated in writing: the dead man "watched." The apparent naïveté of the pattern is deceptive; its peculiar logic, the restraint with which it was applied should not be underrated. It is as if the essence of all imagery, namely that it is life-like yet unchanging, that it is a focus of attention yet out of the reach of purposeful action, gained a new significance. The dead man "present" in effigy shared but did not participate in the activities of life: these on the other hand gained in the face of death a new dignity; they represented for all their triviality the typical, the truly lasting aspects of life.

I have in another context dealt extensively with the development of the so-called "scenes of daily life" in the private tombs of the Old Kingdom.[2] I pointed out that they lack the dramatic import of events, that they are for all their liveliness virtually pictorial concepts: calves being born, cattle fording streams, crops being harvested are part of "husbandry," just as sailors fighting are a typical feature of "boating." The most striking aspect of this unique funereal art is the absence of biographical

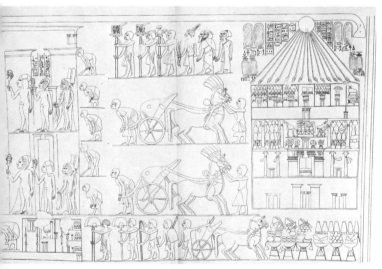

ctorial rendering of actual buildings: Palace and Temple Gate,
om reliefs in a rock tomb at El Amarna, New Kingdom, 1364-1306 B.C.

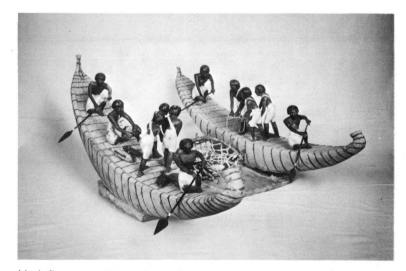

Lively figures to confront the terrifying aspects of death: Fishing craft, painted wood, from the tomb of Mekhetre, New Kingdom, 1364-1306 B.C.

Knife's edge between dramatic
narrative and timeless
statement: Pharaoh defeats
Qadesh and Amod (upper register) and Lybians (lower);
from the Temple of King Seti I
at Abydos, 1304-1209 B.C.

material, of events that would have been "worth telling." The tomb owner was evidently not intended to contemplate the events of his life; on the contrary, transient event was ignored in favor of the typical, the timeless. In fact it must have been the compelling logic of the scheme which prevented the dead man from being drawn more closely into the increasingly lively activities. The meaning of his impassiveness was evidently acknowledged: on a human level the desired union of life and death could only be approximated in an "imaginary" confrontation, the lasting image of the dead contemplating life's ever-recurring activities.

It is precisely because similar preoccupations but totally different solutions were reflected in royal and private tombs that a special difficulty must have arisen when in the reign of Sahure scenic reliefs were introduced in his funerary temple, long after they appeared in the private tombs. This fact in itself may signify a subtle change in the previous all-importance of the pharaoh and may have been related to the rise in importance of the sun god. In the IVth dynasty any pictorial statement had apparently been considered redundant. Now the problem arose how to represent the pharaoh in scenic reliefs. We referred earlier to one form of solution— the king's appearance among gods when performing ritual. These scenes however are lifeless and dull, for the very concept of a divine king atrophies the dramatic tension—so wonderfully evoked in Mesopotamian art—when god and king are confronted. The lively scenes in private tombs must have tempted to a similar display of artistry in the royal tombs. However a pharaoh merely "watching" the typical aspects of life must have been incompatible with his divine office. A solution was found in depicting the king *in actu,* namely either displaying superhuman prowess in typical pursuits, such as hunting, or as the focus of recurring ceremonies, like the display of tribute or of captive enemies. In both cases static perfection, although revealed in acts, transcends actuality. No story was told and all reference to a connection with historic, that is transient event, was avoided.

The scope of a brief essay makes it impossible to pursue in detail the symptoms of this strong, deep-rooted, anti-narrative bias in Egyptian relief and painting or to point out the rare exceptions, the minor heresies indulged in by adventurous artists.[3] The available material from private tombs outweighs by far that from the royal monuments, but the correlation between the two should never be lost sight of. The creed of the immanence of the divine in the person of the pharaoh, the stupendous effort made to affirm this by a monumental denial of his being ephemeral, proved to be— even if undoubtedly shared by his subjects—a tyrannical creed. Its ever-present, dominating manifestation was bound to influence the direction in which artists sought to evoke life-in-death in private tombs, on the level of pharaoh's subjects. It cannot be denied that this meant an opportunity grasped: never again have life's recurring non-events been so lovingly conjured up. But the scope of this art was severely limited; dramatic actuality, whether biographical or historical, was eschewed, even dramatic myth was avoided. A closer

study of royal monuments and private tombs in correlation has shown that changes in the political and religious significance of the pharaoh were reflected in private tombs.

Generally speaking, the pattern of the watching dead confronting lively scenes survived a period of confusion in the late Old Kingdom and of political upheaval thereafter. When pharaonic power was re-established in the Middle Kingdom the scheme suffered only a few heretic onslaughts—one in the form of a pictorial narrative, the transport of a colossus, evidently an important event in the life of the tomb owner.

After the disturbances of the Hyksos period, the by now well-worn scheme came under more insidious attack during the New Kingdom when the secularization of imperial rule and the rising power of the priesthood of Amon altered both the political and the religious status of proud militant pharaohs. Changes were evident in the pattern of private tomb decoration through the intrusion—though on a small scale—of biographical matter and an image of the king as *fons et origo* of bureaucratic power appeared in private tombs for the first time. The rural innocence of Old Kingdom scenes made place for those of sophisticated enjoyment. Nevertheless the pattern survived in the main until the Amarna revolution.

The Amarna period was revolutionary because the king struck at the very roots of his office. Theology had long ago linked the royal function with both the heavens and the under-worlds, but through the identification of the dead king and Osiris it had strong chthonic connotations. Akhenaten monopolized the celestial, rejected the Osirid affiliation. He became the articulate prophet of the divine sun disk, no longer the incarnation of all cosmic powers and as such the source of well-being in the state he ruled. This in itself meant a shift from pharaoh's representative, symbolic character to that of an individual. He stripped himself of the mystery of his office and clearly illustrated his link with the visible sun disk. In short, he turned away from the night side of existence where human faith had for millennia conjured up the consoling mystery of life-in-death. The consequence in scenic art was a complete reversal of the old scheme. Not the typical aspects of life but vibrant actuality, transient event, became its theme. In rock tombs, still tolerated because they offered a ready opportunity for artistic experiment, the "watching" dead disappeared; instead the king often appeared in what became virtually narrative scenes. True, the events depicted were hardly significant occurrences—except in the case of a police officer who recounts in scenes accompanied by text his exploit of catching thieves. The king's acts were limited to visits to the temple or showing himself and his family at the Window of Appearance, but such routine activities gained narrative quality through showing the stages of his journey and his arrival and a number of incidental happenings en route. A remarkable interest was shown in the most "transient" of royal acts: we see the royal family hugging each other, offering flowers, even eating! In short, the Amarna reliefs, barring interesting innovations in the rendering of space and instances of subtle psychological observation, were disappointing from a narrative point of view.

Isolated instance of space-time narrative in Egyptian art: Mahu, Chief of Police (at left) reports to the Vizier and princes of Pharaoh concerning the capture of law-breakers. Bas-relief (detail), rock-tomb at El Amarna, New Kingdom, 1364-1306.

It needed a complete counter-revolution before the potential of the Amarna revolution, its liberation from tradition, could become manifest in a richer form of pictorial narrative. King Seti I showed in his Abydos temple, with its chapels dedicated to the mysteries of Osiris, and with his subterranean cenotaph adjoining it, that he had deliberately reverted to the night side of existence, in the sense that he was deeply concerned with the problem of life-in-death. He did however commemorate his military exploits in a series of splendid reliefs at Karnak. Here his artists achieved a remarkable, and in Egypt unequalled, equipoise between dramatic event and symbolic statement. In the very few instances of earlier New Kingdom efforts to evoke a victorious pharaoh, the paraphernalia of battle are mere stage props. Here in scenes depicting *successive* campaigns, actuality is enhanced by episodic detail. We see towns invested, people fleeing in terror, horses collapsing in the melee; we see the king engaged in hand to hand fight. And yet his towering figure appears to transcend the confusion of battle. The outcome is never in doubt, he represents the superhuman, the divine element of his ancient office. These scenes balanced on a knife's edge between narrative and timeless statement were the last great art inspired by the Egyptian concept of Kingship.

[1]H. Frankfort, *Kingship and the Gods.* Chicago, 1949.
[2]H. A. Groenewegen-Frankfort, *Arrest and Movement,* Faber & Faber, London, 1951.
[3]The most interesting feature of these "heresies" is that they remain isolated instances; they did not start a new development. The battle scene and siege discovered at Deshasheh in Upper Egypt was only once feebly imitated in Saqqara. And in the early New Kingdom, Queen Harshepsut's expedition to Punt, full of delightful episodes, remains an isolated instance. Her having usurped the office of pharaoh (she was the only woman ever to do so) may have caused her to be rather boastful about her expedition.

Duccio's *Jesus Opens the Eyes of a Man Born Blind*, ca. 1310, 17 inches high. This panel is thought to be from the back of Duccio's masterpiece, the *Maestà* altarpiece in the cathedral of Siena. It shows Christ, followed by the 12 apostles, touching the eye of a blind beggar. At right the same beggar, having washed in the pool of Siloam, recovers his sight. National Gallery, London.

By Gregory Martin

Predellas in Siena

A line of Sienese masters continued the medieval narrative traditions in detailed little predella panels which frame their altarpieces with miraculous legends

"Ebbe nella città di Siena excellentissimi et docti maestri..." wrote Lorenzo Ghiberti (1378-1455)—one of the central figures of the Florentine Renaissance. Ghiberti in his *Commentarii* singled out three Sienese excellent and learned masters: Ambrogio Lorenzetti, Simone Martini and Duccio; and indeed our own generation would not quarrel with this roll-call of artists, whose achievements push the city into the forefront of art history.

Their careers span roughly the first half of the fourteenth century. After Lorenzetti's death in 1348 (?), the eloquence of Siena waned. In the following century, perhaps only two artists assumed a more than local significance: Stefano di Giovanni (Sassetta) and Giovanni di Paolo; both are chiefly admired for their retardataire, small-scale narrative pictures, a vein that had, in the hands of their illustrious predecessors, produced works of timeless beauty.

Ghiberti's praise is significant as he could not help but know that Siena's role in creating what was to become the tradition of Western painting was second to that of Florence —the city of Giotto. Not one of Siena's trio could match the stern conviction which led Giotto to destroy inherited artistic fashion and to substitute a new language and grammar based on the reality of observed fact. But the Sienese did have their own dissatisfaction with the accepted (i.e., commonplace) style and the urge to find the means to express the drama of situations vividly and pointedly. And thanks to the highly distinctive personalities of the three men, Siena's contribution was at once more varied and in the short term more widely influential than that of Florence.

The inherited style that was to be replaced had been the creation of the Byzantine Empire. It had satisfied artists and patrons in Italy as a meaningful vehicle for expressing their

Author: Gregory Martin, a curator at the National Gallery, London, specializes in Italian Renaissance painting.

beliefs and passions since the early Dark Ages, which had seen the growth and embellishment of Ravenna. Both the mosaic and then the mural or panel painting conveyed the image of divine majesty and saintliness by a hierarchic language of form, which soon became a passe-partout formula.

The program of this style had been officially accepted at the second Nicene Council, 787, when the cult image which the formula fostered was given the stamp of approval. Its orthodox rationale was made by St. John of Damascus who stated: "the honor shown to the image is transferred to the prototype, and whoever honors an image honors the person represented by it." The program was not accepted without dispute; opposed to it was a Western view of painting which recognized its great didactic potential. As St. Gregory the Great wrote: "One thing is the adoration of an image, another is to learn what to adore from the story rendered by the image. For what the Scripture teaches those who read, this same image shows to those who cannot read but see; because in it even the ignorant see whom they ought to follow, in the image those who do not know letters are able to read."

St. Gregory's concept was to be realized in the decades around 1300 chiefly by Tuscan-born artists. But the impetus had come primarily from Assisi where St. Francis, less than a century previously, had given a new, simple relevance to the message of Christ. The Saint had directed his efforts to inspire and win the faith of ordinary people; in the place of commanding obedience to the mystique of Christ, the Franciscans re-lived the history of His life. And it is in the context of this new attitude to the Gospels that the rejection of the Byzantine style should be seen; not wholly coincidental are the facts that some of the most notable works essaying the new style were decorations of San Francesco Grande in Assisi or the carved embellishment of pulpits—whence the precepts of Christ were uttered—by the Pisani father and son.

Duccio is the first Sienese artist whose extant work shows a meaningful attempt to use painting as a vehicle for dramatic

Simone Martini: *St. Martin Renouncing His Weapons,*
ca. 1325, fresco about 8½ feet high in the church
of S. Francesco Grande, Assisi. Having renounced
his career as a soldier, St. Martin is here shown
denying accusations of cowardice by proposing, to
the astonishment of the Emperor Julian, to meet the
opposing German forces armed only with a cross.

narrative. Ghiberti was fair to state that Duccio *"tenne la
maniere Greca";* but Duccio's Byzantine manner was charged
with a new range of color and enlivened by reference to a
rich dictionary of poses. He is first recorded as active in 1278
in Siena and died some 40 years later, having executed his
greatest work, the *Maestà* for the Duomo of Siena, in 1308-
11.

The *Maestà* is an elaborate extension of the type of cult
image, surrounded by small scenes, which had evolved in the
thirteenth century. But in the very elaboration and scale of the
Madonna and Child surrounded by adoring Saints, Duccio
broke new ground which he made joyously fertile by human-
izing the Christ Child. Duccio's narrative genius was given
full rein in the small scenes on the back which showed episodes of Christ's life, concentrating on His Passion. Here he
required the spectator to read sequentially from scene to
scene, and sought to establish a serial logic for the development of the story by the deliberate repetition of recogniz-
able characters and buildings.

In many instances, Duccio's sense of detail overrides the
demands of the scene as a whole. He is happy to abandon
over-all visual logic to describe an object or an individual's
gesture *per se.* Thus the door giving access to the walled
road leading to Jerusalem and the city gate are each seen
from different angles in *Christ's Entry into Jerusalem*—a
panel on the reverse of the *Maestà.* Yet the multiplicity of
poses—all the result of a deep understanding of man's nature
and behavior—and the concern for archeological accuracy in
costumes and architecture, make Duccio a supreme, instinc-
tive dramatist. He tells the story of Christ healing the man

born blind, also from the reverse of the *Maestà,* with delicacy
and sure-footed passion; the fact that the man is shown twice
is illogical but in terms of the development of the story, entirely appropriate. Duccio's vision encompassed the drama of the
whole and of its constituent parts, but he was not prepared to
submit both to the same logic. The unifying factor is his imaginative intensity.

Duccio had a rich vocabulary but lacked a viable grammar.
In Simone Martini, Siena produced an artist whose style was
immensely influential, but one which lent itself in its rhythmic
fluency more to the creation of eye-seducing pattern than
narrative drama. Simone's personality, however, was sufficiently versatile to make a significant contribution in this direction as well.

He probably developed in the orbit of Duccio; his first
known work, indeed, was the *Maestà* which he frescoed on
the end wall of the Council Chamber of the Palazzo Pubblico
at Siena in 1315. Simone's reputation and popularity soon
won him an international clientele; he was called to work even
further afield than his near-contemporary Giotto, and after
1340 he was summoned to Avignon, where he died in 1344.

The range and variety of Simone's oeuvre is notable; exceptional is his sophisticated adaptability by which he varied
his style to suit his subject matter. Thus in the signed picture
of 1317 showing St. Louis of Toulouse bestowing his crown
on his brother Robert, Simone used forcefully hierarchic
poses and a graceful, dignified articulation of line to convey
the dynastic legitimacy of the Saint's passing on of his
temporal power. Yet in the five predella panels in which were
set out the main elements of a biography of St. Louis, Simone

...ccio's sense of drama and his
...found understanding of human
...avior are brought to bear in
...ry of Christ into Jerusalem,
...anel from the back of the *Maestà*
...Siena. The men in the background
...cutting palm branches which are
...sed forward to the crowd in a
...rling motion that rejoins the
...coming procession of Christ and His
...ciples. 1308-11, 35 7/8 inches high.
...seo dell' Opera del Duomo, Siena.

subjected each scene to the same viewpoint. This degree of coherence was achieved in one step: the five scenes constitute not so much a group of distinct chapters but a book.

Simone's narrative powers are seen at their fullest in the series of frescoes in the chapel of St. Martin, in San Francesco, Assisi, which he executed perhaps about 1330. The decoration of the chapel follows a preconceived plan in which the main elements of each fresco are organized with logical visual reference to each other.

The biography of St. Martin unfolds with graceful clarity. The story line rises in a series of studied gestures and falls with muted eloquence: the drama of each scene is established by sonorous line rather than forceful mass. He brilliantly conveys the amazement of the Roman Emperor, whose adherents are being given money, when the youthful St. Martin, having renounced his career as a soldier, countered accusations of cowardice by proposing to meet the opposing German forces, armed only with a cross.

Simone expressed all the grace and fluency of the Gothic and ensured the popularity of the style for about a century after his death. He is the antithesis of Giotto, despite the sophisticated versatility of his style. Like Duccio, his commitment to the expression of the drama of situations was not total. In fact his most influential creation was the cult image of gentle sweetness embodied in the Madonna of Humility.

Although less known and appreciated today, Ambrogio Lorenzetti was considered by Ghiberti to be a "much better" artist than Simone. This was because of all Sienese artists, his vision was most akin to Giotto's and because his deep interest in the antique anticipated the Renaissance passion for the rediscovery of the achievements of a period that was felt to have prefigured theirs. The influence of classical statues gave Ambrogio's art a weight and evocative poetry which counterbalanced his typically Sienese pleasure in graceful lightness and gentle rhythm.

Ambrogio was probably born in the last decade of the thirteenth century and died presumably a victim of the plague that ravaged much of Europe in 1348. He worked less far afield than Simone, but his range of subject matter was much wider, and shows a breadth unequaled in the fourteenth century. The work that Ghiberti particularly admired is now destroyed; it was described by him as *"una storia picta"*—a *"meravigliosa cosa."*

Enough remains, however, of Ambrogio's work to show the qualities he could bring to bear to create a marvelous painted history. For he not only made a study of the antique, as is shown in some of the figures included in his allegories of Good and Bad Government which he frescoed in the Palazzo Pubblico, Siena in 1338-9, but also had a perceptive eye for the details of the everyday, which brings to life his depictions of Good Government in the Town and in the Country in the same series. These two frescoes present large panoramic views in which people go about their business or make merry. They are encyclopedias of life at the time, in which the sense of space is as far-ranging as a form can allow and as infinite as the eye can see in the country. Indeed, in these frescoes Ambrogio proclaimed that the artist had entirely broken free of the traditions of the Byzantine style—his cur-

Ambrogio Lorenzetti's *Good Government in the Town*, 1338-39, Palazzo Pubblico, Siena.

Ambrogio Lorenzetti:
Presentation in the Temple,
dated 1342, 8 feet 3¼ inches
high. Uffizi Gallery, Florence.

Like its companion fresco in the Palazzo Pubblico, Siena (see p. 126), Ambrogio Lorenzetti's *The Well-Governed Country*
uses an allegorical pretext to present an encyclopedic vision of daily life. Presiding over an assortment of rustic occupations
is the figure of Securitas (upper left) with a banner reading, "Without fear, let each man freely walk, and working let everyone
sow, while such a commune this lady will keep under her rule, because she has removed all power from the guilty.

MERITAB COLOB COPEBIA BENE Z AGLIMIOVI DAB DEBITE PENE

Predellas in Siena

iosity and descriptive eye had discovered a new world of factual reality.

Ambrogio never equaled the emotional intensity of Duccio or the narrative drama of Giotto; but his interests are all those that absorbed the leading artists of the following century. In the Uffizi *Presentation* of 1342 he created the most precisely organized recession of an interior to be executed in the fourteenth century. It was a work sufficiently in advance of his time for Giovanni di Paolo to re-adapt it with only slight modification, just over 100 years later.

The Black Death, which probably killed Ambrogio, had a traumatic effect on Tuscan society and art; confidence temporarily was broken and artists abandoned the spirit of adventure necessary to accomplish powerful narrative pictures. From the observation of human character, the organization of space and accurate rendering of place, artists reverted to the life-saving divine image. And when artists began to pick up the strands some 50 years later, they were Florentines.

The Sienese were content to re-work already charted territory; and thus it is entirely appropriate that one of the most exquisite and evocative of narrative sequences should be the series of predella panels showing the Life of St. Francis by Sassetta. These were executed as part of the high-altarpiece of San Francesco, Borgo San Sepolcro, which Sassetta contracted to paint in 1437 and had completed by 1444, six years before his death, perhaps at the age of 58. Sassetta's style has a pointed, gentle tautness found in a harsher form in his near contemporary, Giovanni di Paolo. His mastery of the language of the previous century was complete; in his hands it became a vehicle for great clarity of expression, as in the *St. Francis Renounces His Earthly Father*, where St. Francis is protected by the bishop from the wrath of his father. Sassetta was hardly interested in current Florentine endeavor to enlarge pictorial space or to establish the solidity of objects within it; spatial relationships were subsidiary to his concern as a story-teller—to which end he brought a direct responsiveness to situations. He was a story-teller *par excellence* but made no great formal advance; this is both the link and the difference between on the one hand Sassetta and Giovanni di Paolo and on the other, the great Sienese masters of the previous century.

Giovanni di Paolo's *Christ Carrying the Cross,* dated 1426, 6 inches high, is the artist's earliest signed work, and shows him continuing the narrative tradition of the preceding century. It is one of five predella panels from an altar of the ecci chapel in the church of S. Domenico, Siena, four of which (including this one) are in the Walters Gallery, Baltimore.

Sassetta: 7 panels from an altarpiece, depicting the life of St. Francis; 34½ inches high; National Gallery, London. The first panel shows the saint as a young soldier giving away his cloak to a poorer knight and receiving from an angel a vision of a celestial castle. Successive panels show him renouncing his earthly father; receiving the Pope's recognition of the Franciscan order; receiving the stigmata; testifying to his Christian faith before the Sultan; shaking the paw of the repentant wolf of Gubbio; and his funeral.

The marriage is arranged,
to the joy of the groom.

The wife tyrannizes and
insults her husband.

The children grow
up wild, like
unpruned trees.

The wife continues to nag even at the table.
In the street, the husband asks advice
of a neighbor how to cure his wife.

The husband drives off into the
nearest wood in order to cut
sticks, his wife still cursing him.

The husband beats off the nine skins of his
wife's viciousness. She dies repentant. The
husband celebrates in a tavern (background).

Philip Fürst publication, Nürnberg, **17th century:** *A Well-Tested and Hallowed Recipe for the Evil Disease of Disobedient Wives.* **British Museum.**

By David Kunzle

The Comic Strip

**Defining an underground medium which for over 400 years
cheerfully and often scatologically has
attacked the virtues and vices of established society**

Study of the history of the comic strip[1] has been bedevilled by the inability or reluctance of writers to agree upon—or even recognize the need for—a workable definition of the term "comic strip." The introductions to those annotated albums of reproductions of twentieth-century strip classics (a dozen or so such works, in various European languages, constitute the bulk of the comic strip "literature") would have us accept as the ancestors of the modern strip such diverse monuments of art as Assyrian reliefs, Parthenon sculptures, Trajan's column, the Bayeux embroidery, Mexican codices and medieval illuminations. If the term "narrative," in the sense the comic strip is narrative, can be made to embrace so vast a range of Western and even non-Western art, we would need to look no farther than our standard art-history surveys. Any useful definition of the comic strip must of course be narrower. I would propose one based upon the following four points:

1. There must be a sequence of distinct but causally interconnected images.

2. There must be a preponderance of image over text (thus excluding book-illustrations).

3. The medium in which the strip appears and for which it was originally intended must be reproductive, i.e. printed, a mass medium.

4. The sequence must tell a story which is new, moral and topical, and which is couched in a popular idiom.

It is noteworthy that the concept of the "comic" does not enter into the above definition; few early strips are comic, either in style or theme, and today by no means the majority

Author: David Kunzle, who received his doctorate under Gombrich at the University of London, is an Assistant Professor at the University of California, Santa Barbara. His *History of the Early Comic Strip* (1450-1826) is being published by the University of California Press.

of strips are comic in intent. Only in the nineteenth century was the strip predominantly comic. The all-embracing term "Comics" for newspaper strip and comic book becomes, especially in the light of Frederick Wertham's research, a tremendous misnomer. Languages other than English do not have this problem; the French say *bande dessinée* (drawn strip), the Italians *fumetto* (literally, little puff of smoke, i.e. balloon—which raises another definitional problem), the Germans *Bilderstreifen* or *Bildergeschichte* (picturestrip, picture story), the Swedes *Seriernas* (serial pictures).

There is also a curious and really quite elementary confusion between "cartoon" and "comic strip." The former term should be restricted to the single-image pictorial gag, which has a history of its own. The early strip does not become cartoon-like, i.e. stylistically caricatural, until relatively late, until the very end of the eighteenth century, in fact. The true ancestors of the modern "comic" are of two kinds: the narrative strip (a subdivided image) and picture story (series of interconnected, but physically non-contiguous images). Both are children of the printing press. They are broadsheets—printed imagery for popular consumption. By the 1460s we find religious broadsheets adopting the subdivided or compartmentalized form which had hitherto been the preserve of the painted altarpiece. They thus break down phase by phase the lives of the saints, the most popular being those who, like Sts. Erasmus and Sebastian, were supposed to have died extravagantly violent and prolonged deaths, and were thus considered good intercessors against physical pain. By the end of the fifteenth century the strip format is being used to tell non-religious, topical stories of war and love: a polemical allegation of host-piercing by the Jews or else a mystical elaboration of the relationship between Christ and the Christian Soul, which turns into an astoundingly sexy—and violent—affair.

The Reformation, which gave a tremendous impetus to pamphleteering and which saw the creation of the first po-

1. Christoph Eysengreisshamer
steals eight pieces of Sacrament.

2. He sells the wafers
to the Jews.

3. The Jews take them
to their synagogue.

4. They stab the wafers
and make them bleed.

5. They send four pieces to
other Jewish communities.

6. They burn the Host: the Christ
Child, angels and doves appear.

7. The Jews
are arrested.

8. The Jews are beheaded (ritual
execution in remainder of strip).

**Part of a broadsheet published in Nürnberg
in the 1490s: *A Horrible Story
of What the Jews Did at Passau* (1477).**

**Surviving fragments of a German
broadsheet, *The Courtship of Jesus
and the Christian Soul,* ca. 1470.**

Jesus tries to wake the Soul,
who wishes to stay asleep.

Jesus gives the Soul a love-potion. The Soul
seeks for Jesus, who hides behind a curtain.

litical cartoons, had relatively little direct influence on the development of the broadsheet strip. There is a hardening of political-religious lines in polemical imagery, which Luther and Cranach between them pushed to a degree of the grotesque and vulgar such as only the underground cartoonist of today is beginning to emulate. The broadsheet strip acquires in the course of the sixteenth and seventeenth centuries another function: that of documentary analysis of political repression. This is basically of two kinds. First, there is the massacre print, which accumulates military atrocities; second, there is the plot print, which attempts the pictorially more taxing task of tracing the stages of some plot or intrigue against a newly independent government or religion. The massacre strip runs like a bloody red line throughout the seventeenth century, that most war-ridden of centuries before our own. It constitutes a fearful indictment of Catholic-Habsburg tyranny, starting with the Spanish Fury in Antwerp, 1576, continuing with Dutch exposure of Spanish oppression throughout the world and other Catholic attempts to exterminate alien religions—Prague 1621, Palatinate 1630s, Piedmont 1655, France 1685-86. The Revocation of the Edict of Nantes, ordered by Louis XIV on the last date, provoked what must be considered the most impressive and frightening of this category of highly political and most "uncomic" strips. The etching is by a little-known Dutchman called Romeyn de Hooghe, who became self-appointed (and unpaid) cartoonist in the cause of William III, both as Prince of Orange and later as King of England. His style has something of the ferocity of Rubens, and appears all the more arresting after the rather drab, workaday realism of his German and Dutch predecessors.

The "plot prints" relate Catholic attempts to subvert Protestant governments, notably in Prague, 1617-19, and in London, 1678-79 (Popish Plot). The massive, artfully contrived and excessively successful (because ultimately counterpro-

ductive) publicity campaign mounted by the Whigs to expose various real and alleged "Horrid Hellish Popish Plots," gave rise to a series of packs of political playing cards. These cards trace, in the suit reproduced for instance, an episode which is still one of the great unsolved mysteries of history.

To various anonymous or little-known Dutch and English engraver-publishers goes the credit for achieving a breakthrough in the art of pictorial narrative during the last third of the seventeenth century. They are no longer content to list the external circumstances, and the crasser physical manifestations of a political event, but try to link causes and effects, establish antecedents, and pinpoint pictorially each successive stage in an orderly, succinct and comprehensive manner. Without resorting to speech balloons (a rarity in strips at all times until our own, although standard equipment of the cartoonist), with a minimum of caption, the little pictures alone bear the brunt of a complex narrative. While Romeyn de Hooghe persists in the "Baroque" tradition of filling each scene with several episodes, the English engraver preserves an analytical logic by restricting each scene to one episode. The time-span between them is also more narrow and carefully measured.

Meanwhile, a parallel development was taking place in the broadsheet picture story, which frequently abandoned the larger political arena in order to influence personal morality. Italian and German strips and narrative sequences on various human follies and vices elaborated the old medieval schemes of the Seven Deadly Sins and the Ten Commandments. Germans (particularly Nurembergers) in the seventeenth century seemed to have felt strongly about the place of women in marriage, and delighted in strips which are half humorous-farcical, and half cruel-tragic, showing wives who dominate their husbands and family, get soundly punished for it, and have the Nine Skins of Evil stripped off their backsides. The female sin of Pride paled, however, before a worse one: that

Jesus tries to bribe the Soul to leave Him alone. The Soul hears secrets from Jesus.

The Soul and Jesus are reunited. Jesus entices the Soul with violin music.

Jesus disillusions the Soul with earthly things. Jesus strips the soul naked.

of Lechery. A gynocracy was bad, but death from venereal disease was worse. In sixteenth-century Italy there are numerous ballad and pamphlet illustrations revealing the horror of the French malady; in northern Europe at this time, artists showed a predilection for illustrations for and variations on the Prodigal Son parable. During the following century, these twin currents flowed into a broader river of regular cautionary tales replete with grim details upon the fate of the lecher who consorts with whores, and the life of the girl who rises to the privileged status of a Venetian courtesan, only to descend to the lowest degradation, and die smitten with poverty and disease.

It was tales such as these that William Hogarth (1697-1764) elevated into a form which is both broadsheet narrative, and artistically comparable to the achievements of the great social commentators of all time—Brueghel, Callot, Goya and Daumier. Eschewing the strip format, which would not have left him scope for narrative enrichment, Hogarth took most of the known broadsheet themes—the dangers of harlots, rakes, pimps, mercenary marriage, idleness and cruelty, and composed his stories with something of the satirical verve and detail of a comic novelist, such as his friend and admirer, Henry Fielding. While the number of scenes to each of his five major picture stories (6, 8, 6, 12 and 4) tends to be smaller than in the broadsheets, the compositions are larger and throbbing with incidental detail, both in the settings and the subsidiary characters.

His was a unique (and commercially successful) achievement, which many tried to emulate. In France Jean-Baptiste Greuze managed, with much momentary popular applause, narrative situations adumbrated over two large, overloaded and over-sentimental scenes. His public however did not permit him, as the English did Hogarth, to enter into the life of the vicious and depraved, without which the picture-story can barely sustain interest. In Germany, Daniel Chodowiecki (a curious figure, never much regarded outside his own country) performed the feat of condensing the Hogarthian story into a sequence of calendar illustrations, which in their tiny format (2 by 1½ inches) have an elegance and sparkle lacking in the rugged engravings of Hogarth. At the turn of the century, in yet another part of Europe, we have to consider the enigmatic figure of Goya, who can never be conveniently packaged into any history of art, and much of whose graphic art is perched in the most vexing fashion on the very edge of the "moralizing picture story." His *Caprices* and *Disasters of War* are not arranged haphazardly; a theme develops, but it is of a philosophical, rather than directly cause-and-effect nature. His "story" of folly and cruelty in social relationships or in warfare unfolds not in an ordered sequence, like eighteenth- or nineteenth-century fiction, but with multiple twists and turns, digressions, reversions and interlacings more reminiscent of Joyce. Goya's etchings were not, moreover, popular at all—the *Caprices* reached only a few friends and connoisseurs, and the *Disasters of War* were not published until a generation after the artist's death.

Various attempts to incorporate Hogarthian narrative into existing, socially respectable categories of art, such as history painting or literary illustration, failed. It was not until the last decade of the century that the necessary stylistic transformation occurred, which gave a new lease on life to the old moral picture-story, turning it into the witty, caricatural strip. The formal revolution of caricature, an art nurtured in the studios of a number of seventeenth-century Italian artists, was first given political force by English party factionalism in the course of the eighteenth century. The names associated with the caricatural strip during the so-called Golden Age of Caricature pale before those of Gillray and Rowlandson, the master-cartoonists (i.e. producers of single-scene caricatures). Who has heard of Henry Bunbury, George "Mustard" Woodward, John Nixon, Charles Williams, etc.—and Richard Newton? The latter died at the age of 21, leaving behind a hilarious set of social satires. These are true comic strips—light and grotesque in line and narrative tone, but also often imbued with a tragic quality which marks the artist as the last of the Hogarthians. Newton and the handful of his colleagues helped to leaven the ponderous morality which was the legacy of Hogarth with a sense for the absurd.

The absurdist element is the stylistic hallmark of the father of the modern comic strip, the Swiss Rodolphe Töpffer (1799-1846), a writer and artist who is at last beginning to receive the critical attention he deserves.[2] The protagonists of his strips are neither villains nor heroes, but a species of anti-hero

Plot print, attributed to Francis Barlow: *The Popish Plot,* 1679. Spades suit from a pack of cards pinpointing events in the murder of Justice Edmund Bury Godfrey. British Museum.

Massacre print: *Spanish Tyrannies in the West Indies and the Netherlands,* Dutch, ca. 1623. The layout is typical of many 17th-century political broadsheets: narrative border surrounding an allegory, here the ram of divine vengeance destroying the Tower of Castile (i.e., Spain). Van Stolk Collection.

The rake returns to a prostitute.

Ill with the French disease (syphilis).

Takes to begging.

Sleeps under a butcher's bench.

Accepts broth from the Friars.

Dies miserably.

Callisto Ferrante publication, Rome, 1611: *The Miserable Life of Those Who Consort with Prostitutes,* bottom half of a broadsheet. Bibliothèque Nationale, Paris.

Romeyn de Hooghe: *Tyrannies against the Huguenots in France,* 1685-86, scenes from a broadsheet arranged like *Spanish Tyrannies,* p. 137. Van Stolk Coll.

Camps out at night.

Is buried in an unmarked vault.

who struggles desperately, fruitlessly and farcically against the caprices of fate, nature and (less often) society. They are buffeted through the pages of his little oblong albums (the bigger ones contain close to 100 pages), fleeing from passionate fiancées, roaring lions and automated policemen. On one page they quietly chase butterflies, on the next they are tossed into the sky by a whirlwind—to land eventually in the mouth of a whale, the stem of a telescope, or in the midst of a hayrick. Caught in a never-ending series of fantastic disasters and dilemmas, they are apt to seek respite—by changing their underclothes. The adventures of Töpfferian heroes are purposefully purposeless, flow with calculated non-sequiturs, and, like a Sterne novel, make digression into a narrative principle. The pace is sustained by a minor revolution of draftsmanship, for Töpffer first discovered how to turn systematic doodling to account, how to exploit the accident, and how to vary physiognomies experimentally. He made broken lines more suggestive than continuous ones, and by abandoning the academic concept of three-dimensional, anatomical drawing, he learned how to render movement. His art is all movement, breathless, relentless: it is movement for movement's sake. The fixed relationship between cause and effect, which had underpinned all the old crime-and-punishment strips, becomes mobile to the point of disintegration. Traditional concepts of morality yield their supremacy to the irrational and the comic.

Like Hogarth, Töpffer was widely imitated, and with about as much success. His style and his subjects were plagiarized and borrowed by numerous cartoonists working for the periodical industry. The comic strip thus entered journalism, where caricature and cartoon have been lodged—for better,

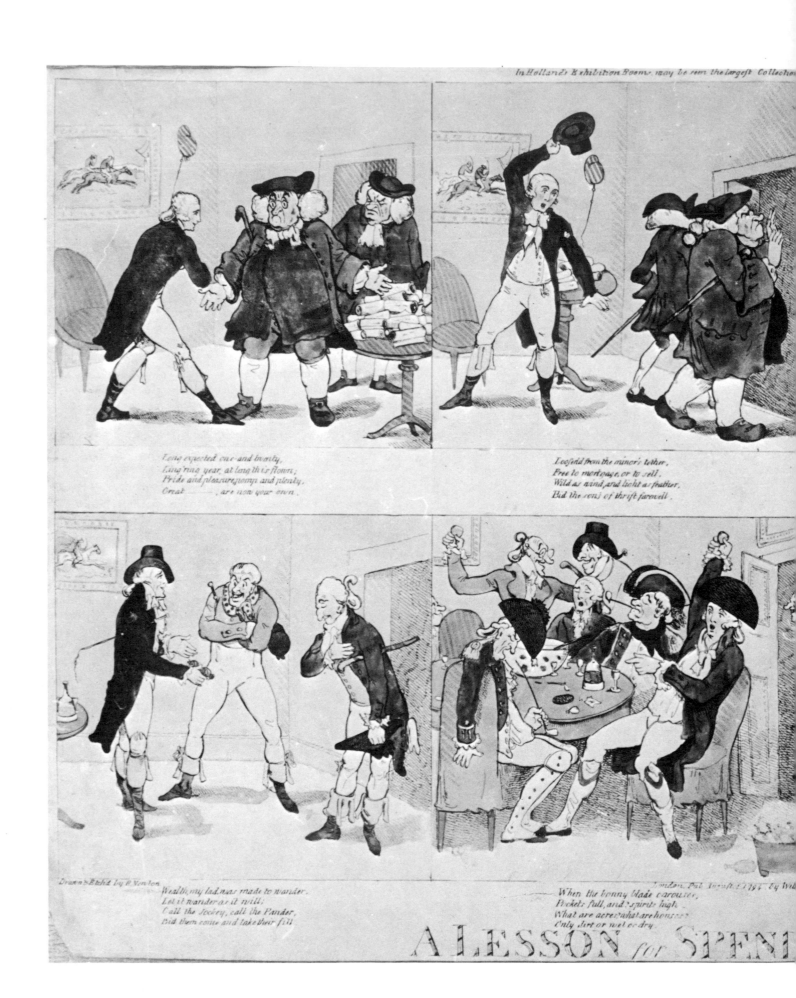

Long expected one-and-twenty,
Ling'ring year, at length is flown;
Pride and pleasure, pomp and plenty,
Great _____, are now your own.

Loos'd from the minor's tether,
Free to mortgage, or to sell,
Wild as wind, and light as feather,
Bid the sons of thrift farewell.

Drawn & Etch'd by R. Newton

Wealth, my lad, was made to wander,
Let it wander as it will;
Call the Jockey, call the Pander,
Bid them come and take their fill.

London, Pub. August 1794. By Will

When the bonny blade carouses,
Pockets full, and spirits high,
What are acres, what are houses?
Only dirt or wet or dry.

A LESSON for SPEN

The Comic Strip

Call the Betsies, Kates, and Jennies,
All the names that Lauity can;
Lavish of your grandsire's guineas,
Shew the spirit of an heir.

All that prey on vice or folly
Joy to see their quarry fly;
There the Gamester, light and Jolly,
There the Lender grave and sly.

Should the guardian friend or mother,
Tell the woes of wilful waste;
Scorn their counsel, scorn their pother,
You can hang or drown at last.

THRIFTS — *by Dʳ JOHNSON*

The old moral picture-story turns into the witty, caricatural
strip: Richard Newton's *A Lesson for Spendthrifts*, 1794 (British
Museum). 1. The spendthrift inherits. 2. He rejects his guardians.
3. Revels with prostitutes. 4. Gambles. 5. Engages a jockey and a
pander. 6. Carouses. 7. Spurns mother and guardian. 8. Suicide.

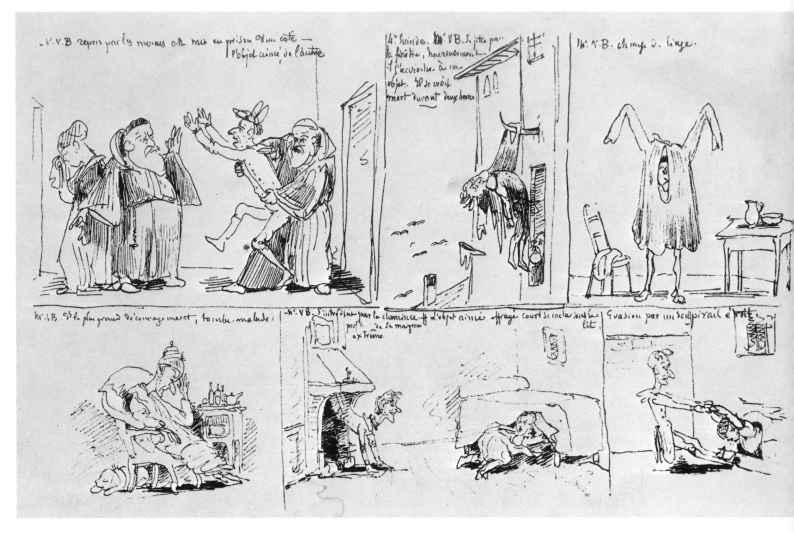

Adventures of M. Vieux-Bois, 1827, by the father of the modern comic strip, the Swiss Rodolphe Töpffer. Here the farcical hero is captured by monks who believe him to be from outer space and therefore a pagan. He is imprisoned and separated from his beloved. There follows a ludicrous attempt at suicide; as always he takes respite by changing his underclothes. He becomes discouraged and falls sick. Finally he reaches his beloved and rescues her.

for worse—ever since. Various small French and English satirical magazines published Töpfferian strips, without making any really positive contribution. The lightness of Töpffer's line hardens; the sublime absurdity of his characters and situations turns to conventional comedy.

It was in Germany, where caricature had never become really acclimatized as in England and France, that the next step was taken. Wilhelm Busch was equally adept as popular poet and comic draftsman. His continuous success, from the 1860s until his death in 1908, depends in part on his brilliantly easy, jingly verse, and partly on his no less facile sense for linear rhythms. Busch is remembered chiefly for the gratuitously and ingeniously sadistic activities of Max and Moritz, youthful mischief-makers of a kind that has formed a staple of popular humor ever since. The psychological significance of Busch's subject-matter (which embraces, of course, much more than monster-children) and of his deep-rooted philosophical cynicism has yet to be defined; but the esthetic impact of his art for the future development of the comic strip is clear: Caran d'Ache brought the diagrammatic clarity

and exquisite economy of his line to France, and Richard Outcault (on the instigation of William Randolph Hearst, a Busch-lover as a child) incorporated it, in a rougher, homespun version, into the American newspaper. It was a style perfectly adapted to the simple farce and the basically physical, familiar domestic situations demanded by the readers of the Sunday supplements. Töpfferian surrealism and his delicate psychology seem to have been left far behind. What one may term the metaphysical slapstick of many nineteenth-century strips has become mechanical slapstick—proto-Disney. The draftsmanship too will soon tend to the mechanical, and over-production on the part of individual artists will be the rule. The balloon, long resisted as an esthetic obtrusion, now reigns uncontested, to eke out a basic pictorial inadequacy as much as to flesh out the story-line.

This is not the place even to outline the daunting proliferation of the comic strip in our own century. Suffice it to say that intellectuals today share a widespread feeling that newspaper strips today are a poor reflection of American society, or else an all-too-accurate reflection of an unreflective

Daniel Chodowiecki's condensation of the Hogarthian story into a series of tiny calendar illustrations (2 by 1½ inches): *The Life of a Rake* (final six scenes from a sequence executed for the *Berlin Calendar,* 1774). British Museum.

society. In a country torn by racial strife, anti-war dissent, the drug-problem and attempts at sexual liberation, where are these issues to be found in the comics page? The best we have is the liberal-intellectual paranoia of a Charlie Brown, or (more significant, I think) the sporadic political jibes which are beginning to make themselves felt in *Pogo, the Wizard of Id*, and *B.C.* The host of militarist, conservative, soap-opera and escapist humor strips continues to prosper—but not, one hopes, forever.

The subterranean reaction has set in. The recent flurry of underground newspapers has helped to launch a whole network of "hippie" arts, including strips which combine the satirical, the pornographic and the psychedelic. A major journal of the "establishment underground" (overground underground?), the *Evergreen Review*, which consists of an intelligent mix of politics, social-comment and sex, has launched an anti-Wonder-Woman through the subterranean skies—Phoebe Zeitgeist. She seems to be less a satire on a sexually perverted America than a parody of the sex-and-sadism comic

book. She may also serve to explain how it is the U.S. public can take in their stride disclosures of torture and massacre in Vietnam. The truly underground comic is heralded by *Zap Comix*, upon which various noted San Francisco Bay area artists have collaborated. Best known is Robert Crumb, who may be described as a freaked-out Disney. The pornographic character of much of his work (at least, that portion of it periodically seized from the Berkeley Print Mint, his principal outlet) is self-evident. Is it a Surrealistic put-down of the popular "straight" pornographic magazine—or is it a satirical send-up of our own erotic fantasies? There is also a concealed political element, which is more visible to those inclined to view as subversive to Capitalist Government and High Art any gesture which might *épater le bourgeois*. It is hard to form an immediate opinion of Crumb, because his narrative line is rather foggy, and his draftsmanship tends to the diffuse. Often, he is superbly funny. Stylistically, there is little relationship with the art of that supreme master of the underground cartoon, Ron Cobb, who is as fastidious in his

Parody of sex-and-sadism entertainment: *Adventures of Phoebe Zeit-geist*, Episode 3, 1968, written by Michael O'Donoghue, drawn by Frank Springer. From the Evergreen Review (Grove Press, New York).

A page of Robert Crumb's *Hairy*, in Zap Comix No. 3, 1968. The Print Mint, Berkeley, California.

Post-Disney Surrealism: a page of Rick Griffin's strip in Zap Comix No. 2, 1968. The Print Mint, Berkeley.

line as he is in the conception of the drawings. Unless Cobb is to turn strip cartoonist (which seems unlikely), Jules Feiffer will remain the unchallenged exponent of the radical strip. The pictorial interest of his art is real, but limited; that of psychedelic illustration and poster-art potentially is unlimited, and it is in this style that I would expect some new development in the narrative strip. What Leary terms the "retinal orgasm" of psychedelic art may, on the other hand, be more attuned to escapist psycho-erotic fantasies than to radical protest. To achieve the latter in the comic strip requires no more than a return to the role it played in earlier centuries, and a comparable degree of stylistic realism.

1 The author is preparing a comprehensive volume, *The History of the Early Comic Strip (ca. 1450-1826),* to be published shortly by the University of California Press.
2 Eppie Wiese, *Enter the Comics. Rodolphe Töpffer's Essay on Physiognomy.* University of Nebraska Press, 1965.

Narrative Art

Index of Illustrations

Page numbers in italics indicate colorplates

Credits

Cover: photograph by Eric Pollitzer. Colorplates on pp. 11, 14-15, 18, 27, 87, 90, 107, 127, from Mondadori, Verona. 30: G. P. Putnam's Sons. 33: David S. Brooke. 70: Lund Humphries Publishers Ltd., London. 72, 76, 77, 78, 82, 83: Joan Lebold Cohen. 74, 78, 79, 80, 81: Van Erp, Indonesian Archeological Survey. 106: BBC Publications, London. 114: Flinders Petrie, *Deshasheh.* 117, 121: Norman de G. Davies, *El Amarna IV.* 117: Metropolitan Museum. 118: The Oriental Institute, Chicago.

A.P.F., Inc.

SHOWROOMS:
231 East 60 Street
&
1001 Madison Avenue

FACTORY & OFFICE:
315 East 91 Street
New York City

(TEL. for N.Y. Office)
212 - LE4-6400

Master Framemakers & Conservators

Art Book Festival

New Publications from Here and Abroad

THE SAN FRANCISCO I LOVE

Photographs by Peter Fink, Text by Joyce Peterson
Intro. by Mayor Joseph L. Alioto.

Magnificent kaleidoscope that will be treasured both as an American keepsake and a prize example of the photographer's art. Peter Fink trained his camera with loving insight on the people and places, sights, tempo and tastes bringing into focus the indelible character that has made it the most captivating of all American cities. This is a panoramic portrait that includes every place of historic and artistic interest. 130 stunning photographs, 12 in color. 9½" x 10½". **$8.95**
After Christmas $9.95

PICASSO'S THIRD DIMENSION

Photographs and Text by Gjon Mili

The noted "humanist-with-camera" presents new ways of looking at Picasso's three-dimensional art, and at the wiry old magician himself. This is a sensational picture record of two visits with Picasso, 18 years apart. 132 dramatic photos, 72 in full color. One recent visit describes and depicts Picasso's inner sanctum studio-home at Mougins, the repository of never-before-seen sculptures, collages and ceramics. The other visit, at Vallauris, records the now famous series of light drawings Picasso created with a flashlight. 9" x 12". **$27.50**

SPANISH FURNITURE

By Louis Feduchi

This huge, lavishly illustrated volume is a "must" for collectors and dealers in antiques, for art historians and museum curators. In 269 carefully chosen photographs — 53 in brilliant color — the origins, evolution, design and decoration of Spanish furniture is traced through all its periods. Text in English, Spanish, French and German. 10¼" x 11". **$25.00**

XXe Siecle No. 35 — Panorama '70

The newest issue of the famous French annual, copies of which become instant collectors' items. Contains an ORIGINAL color lithograph by Marc Chagall; an ORIGINAL lithograph by Soulages; 20 full-color plates and 166 halftone reproductions; fourteen illustrated articles on the major exhibitions of the year. Among the most important are critical reviews of the Met's New York Painting and Sculpture 1940-1970 by Pierre Courthion and A. B. Nakov, Chagall's Apotheosis, by San Lazzaro plus articles on Magnelli, Manessier, Gentilini, Roberta Crippa, etc. Text is in French, with an appendix in English summarizing each article. 9½" x 12½". **$17.50**

JOAN MIRO

Intro. by James Johnson Sweeney
Photos by Joaquim Gomis,
Catala-Roca, and
Repro-color Llovet

The extraordinary faithfulness to color reproduction in this book has to be seen to be believed. Over 240 full-page color plates present Miro's masterpieces from early Cézannesque and Fauve works to his mature murals, paintings and sculptures. 8¼" x 8¼", beautifully printed and bound in Barcelona. **$22.50**

THE CHATEAUX OF THE LOIRE I LOVE

By Philippe du Puy de Clinchamps
Photos by Leo Pellisier, et al

Intro. by Maurice Genevois. This lovely volume takes you on a tour of these famous castles, palaces, retreats and fortresses — the pride of French architecture and history. Every important chateau is described and depicted, from Amboise to the three great C's — Chambord, Chenonceaux, Chaumont-to Villandry. 130 spectacular photographs, 12 in color. 9½" x 10½". **$8.95**
After Christmas $9.95

ART OF THE JAPANESE OBJECT

By Maria L. Borras
Photos by Takeji Lwamiya

The utility, economy and simplicity which are the inherent qualities of Japanese objects are exceeded only by their "spontaneous" forms and purity of design. Following an incisive aesthetic analysis, 116 plates, 32 in ravishing color, reproduce the best of Japanese dolls and marionettes; baskets, casks and bowls; kimonos, fans and parasols; and much more. Text in English, Spanish, French and German. 8½" x 8½". **$12.50**

HOMAGE TO MATISSE

Special issue of the
Review XXe Siecle
Edited by G. Di San Lazzaro

32 plates in color, 150 illustrations in b. & w. With a linocut reproduction (suitable for framing) of an original created by Henri Matisse for the 1938 issue of the Review. Published in conjunction with the Grand Palais Exhibition (the international art event of the year). This biographical-critical homage is an indispensable source book on the history of modern art. 19 critics assess every facet of his career. 8½" x 11". **$15.00**

COMPLETE WORKS OF MARINO MARINI

Ed. by G. Di San Lazzaro, and
with essays by Sir Herbert Read,
Patrick Waldberg and others.

A major publication devoted to the paintings, graphics and sculpture of one of the world's foremost living artists, acclaimed not only for his brilliant handling of color but for the powerful eroticism and spirituality of his themes. Representative works are reproduced in 68 magnificent hand-tipped plates, mostly full-page and all in faithful color. A huge, luxuriously produced volume that is bound to cause a stir in the art world. 10" x 14". **$50.00**

GIACOMETTI: THE COMPLETE GRAPHICS

By Herbert Lust
Intro. by John Lloyd Taylor

353 illustrations, 70 full-page reproductions. Lithographs, etchings and book illustrations — virtually all of Giacometti's majestic achievement in graphics — are beautifully reproduced in this volume. It also contains the only comprehensive, illustrated catalogue raisonné of Giacometti's graphic works, with a critical analysis of his œuvre. Catalogue raisonné. 9" x 12". **$25.00**

MARC CHAGALL: DRAWINGS AND WATER COLORS FOR THE BALLET

By Jacques Lassaigne

This lavish volume is the first to reproduce the bold, breathtakingly beautiful original designs for Aleko, The Firebird, and Daphnis and Chloe. Included are décor and costumes; sketches for dancers, monsters, gypsies, animals, magicians; and the vast, fabulous sets which transformed these ballets into magical melanges of flowers, mystical birds and floating cities. Thirteen double-page color reproductions, 68 plates in color, plus one original color lithograph suitable for framing. Beautifully printed in France by Mourlot Freres. 10½" x 14". Special import. **$37.50**

HOMAGE to MARC CHAGALL

Edited by G. Di San Lazzaro

26 color plates, 160 illustrations in black and white, and with a reproduction, suitable for framing, of an original Chagall lithograph, created for this special issue of Review XXe Siecle. Biographical-critical appreciations and a pictorial summary of a remarkable career. Same format as the Matisse volume. 8½" x 11". **$12.50**

At bookstores or from:

Tudor Publishing Co.
572 Fifth Avenue, New York, N. Y. 10036

AQUATEC, THE ARTISTS ACRYLIC

Water based. Deep. Brilliant. Permanent. Aquatec is the world's finest acrylic artist color. Made of 100% acrylic polymer emulsion that makes it possible for artists to explore new and expressive techniques from delicate, transparent washes, to heaviest impasto. **Special Introductory Offer:** a working palette of 11 studio-size colors, plus Aquatec Jel and a King-size tube of Titanium White, only $7.75.* Check or money-order...no COD's. For color chart and full information write Bocour Artist Colors, Inc. 552 West 52 Street, New York 10019. (In Canada, Heinz-Jordan Ltd., 42 Gladstone Rd., Toronto 3.) Aquatec is available at leading art supply stores everywhere.   *NYC residents add 6% Sales Tax.

dubuffet
hourloupe paintings & sculpture

november the j.l.Hudson gallery 1206 woodward, detroit

More new
and exciting books from Abrams
for fall 1970

M. KNOEDLER & CO

Old Masters • Impressionists • American Art • Modern Masters

LOUISE BOURGEOIS	HENRY MOORE
SALVADOR DALI	ERNST WILHELM NAY
VIEIRA DA SILVA	BARNETT NEWMAN
WILLEM DE KOONING	EMIL NOLDE
DUCHAMP-VILLON	MAURICE PRENDERGAST
ARSHILE GORKY	BERNARD ROSENTHAL
ETIENNE HAJDU	TONY SMITH
VASSILY KANDINSKY	PIERRE SOULAGES
BERTO LARDERA	BRAM VAN VELDE

Cable address "Knoedler" NEW YORK, 14 East 57th Street
PARIS, 85bis Faubourg St. Honoré • LONDON, 34 St. James's Street

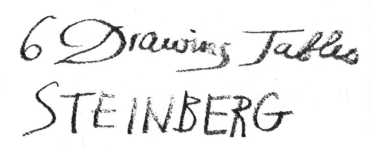

164

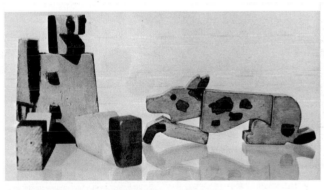